Mother of Freedom

ALSO BY BEN Z. ROSE

John Stark: Maverick General

Mother of Freedom

Mumbet and the Roots of Abolition

Ben Z. Rose

TreeLine Press
Lincoln, Massachusetts

Designed and composed in Ehrhardt MT Pro
at Hobblebush Books, Concord, New Hampshire
(www.hobblebush.com)
Printed in the United States of America

First edition copyright 2009
Second edition copyright 2020

Publisher's Cataloging-In-Publication Data
(Prepared by The Donohue Group, Inc.)

Rose, Ben Z.

Mother of freedom : Mumbet and the roots of abolition / Ben Z. Rose. — 2nd ed.

p. : map ; cm.

Includes bibliographical references and index.

ISBN: 978-0-9789123-3-8

1. Freeman, Elizabeth, 1744?–1829. 2. Women slaves—Massachusetts—Biography. 3. Slaves—Emancipation—Massachusetts. 4. Free African Americans—Massachusetts. 5. Slavery—New England—History—18th century. I. Title.

E444.F87 R67 2008

973.3/092 B 2008907571

Published by:

TreeLine Press
Lincoln, Massachusetts

For bulk purchases, contact
Pathway Book Services (pathwaybook.com)

In memory of my grandmothers,
Etta Rose and Sylvia Burgin

Contents

Note to the Second Edition

As I discovered in my first book, *John Stark: Maverick General*, reconstructing events that concern people who lived two hundred years ago presents numerous challenges. Mumbet, as far as we know, did not read or write. Thus, there are no personal letters to peruse. Furthermore, birth and marriage records of black slaves in New England were exceedingly rare. In the case of Mumbet, we cannot even determine exactly where and when she was born. Photography did not exist in her time. It would not be for another nine years after her death that Louis Daguerre captured the first image of a human form, in 1838. Paintings and portraits of black slaves of the eighteenth century are rare, and we must rely on our imagination to visualize what Mumbet may have looked like at nearly all stages of her life.

We are fortunate that Mumbet's chief chronicler, Catharine Maria Sedgwick, was one of America's earliest, most prolific, and celebrated novelists. Her passion and reverence for Mumbet are recorded both loyally and lovingly. As I reviewed the primary and secondary sources available to piece together Mumbet's story, I found areas of ambiguity. After taking a deep breath and pausing periodically to reflect on the challenges involved in accurately interpreting an historical record with known gaps, I finally accepted the idea that certain facts relating to her life may never be known. It does not, in my mind, diminish her achievements, or detract from telling her story.

Like Aramita Ross, who selected the name Harriet Tubman after gaining her freedom, Mumbet also chose a new name—Elizabeth Freeman—upon winning hers. However, the Sedgwick children's reverence for Mumbet, who became a second mother to them, meant that she would be known by that name, out of affection, for the rest of her life. The spelling of her name has taken several forms over time with the most common being Mumbet and Mum Bett. In an effort to help rally around a single spelling, I have adopted 'Mumbet' in the subtitle of the book in this new edition. I have however kept the multiple spellings of her name throughout the book, as an homage to the literature and source material I encountered during my research.

Please see the Afterword to this book for more information about my relationship to the story of Mumbet.

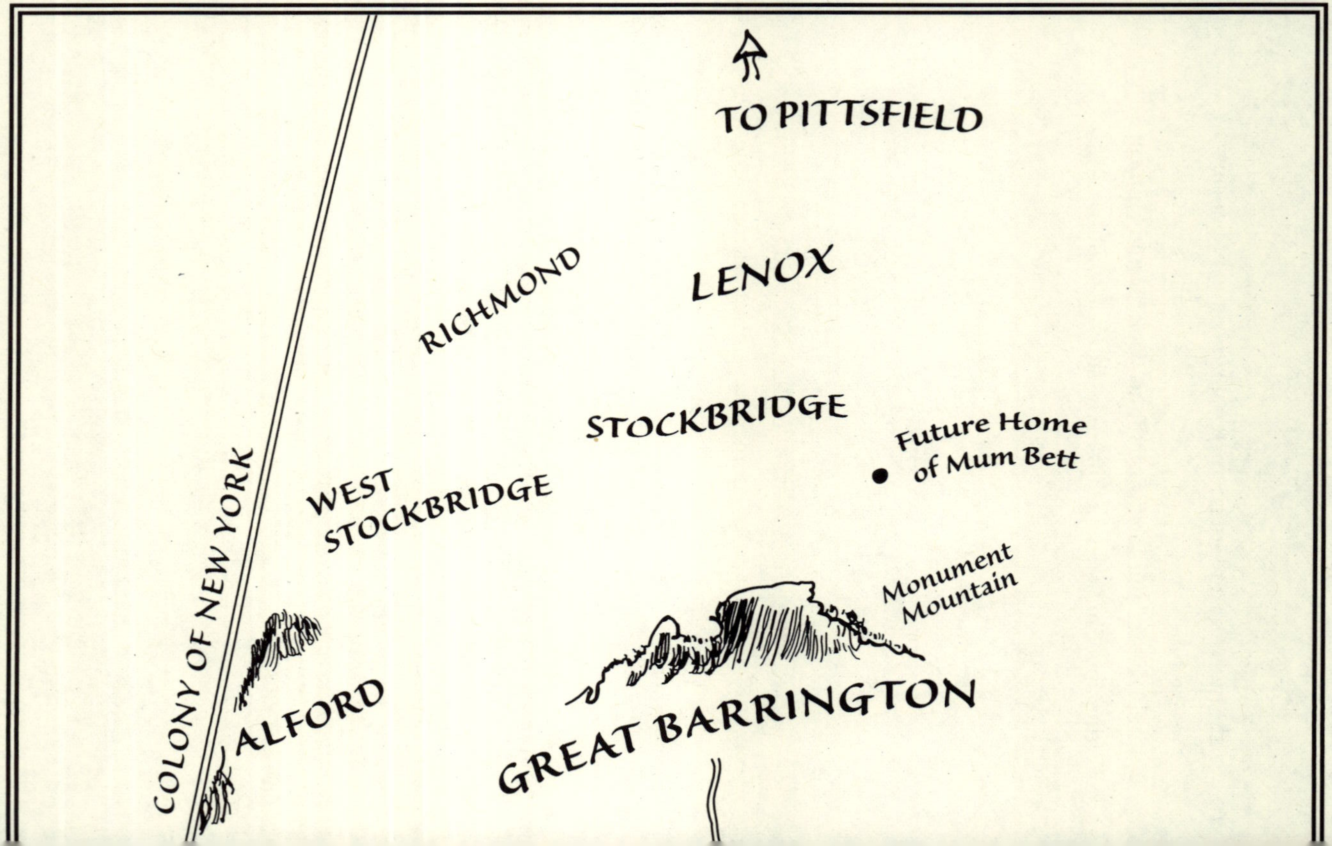
TO PITTSFIELD
RICHMOND
LENOX
STOCKBRIDGE
Future Home
of Mum Bett
WEST
STOCKBRIDGE
COLONY OF NEW YORK
Monument
Mountain
ALFORD
GREAT BARRINGTON

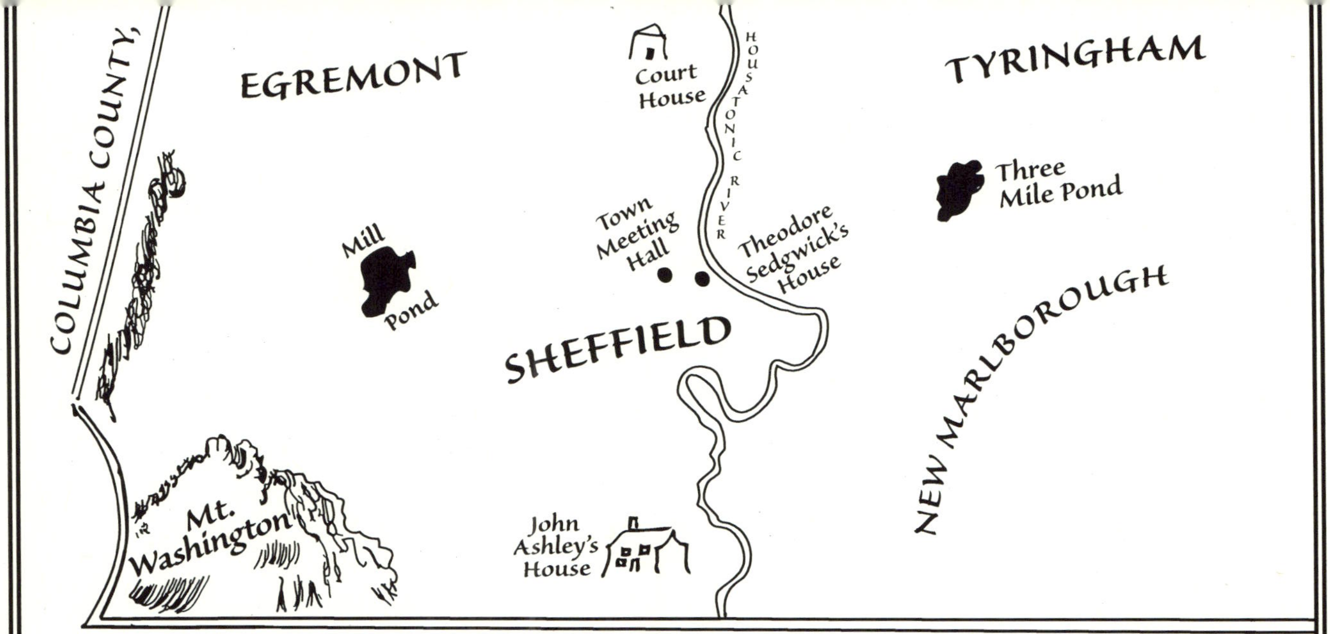

Southwest Berkshire County, *circa* 1775
Massachusetts Bay Colony

Pain and Promise

A breeze blew through a crack in her bedroom window. It sent a shiver up her spine. She watched as a thin veneer of ice began to form on the glass which lit her room faithfully. If only for a moment, the chill took her mind off her great burden. Her broad shoulders shrugged slightly as she stepped back from the window to sit on the bed. She thought about her overbearing mistress. She thought about her sister Lizzie, and about the shackles that bound them to their fate.

Her real name, we suspect, was Elizabeth, but as a girl, she was nicknamed Bett or Betty. Her name had changed again when the children she watched over began to call her Mumbet. Though she never learned to read or write, her name was sometimes written by others as two words, or, as it was on her epitaph, a single word, Mumbet. Black slaves of the eighteenth century often lost their surname, for the simple reason that many, like Mumbet, had been separated from their parents, and sold into bondage, thus losing whatever link existed to their family.

On the eve of the American Revolution in 1775, Mumbet was about thirty years old. She was already known for her compassion and expertise as a midwife, and for her skill in helping raise the four children of her master and mistress. Mumbet was kind-hearted and quick-witted. She was an incredibly strong woman who, when she put her foot down, "kept it down."[1]

Bett was well aware of the promise of freedom contained in the Sheffield Resolves, a pact signed by the leading citizens of her community, among them her owner, John Ashley. She had served Ashley and his colleagues their meals in his home during the sessions which led to the signing of the document. By "keeping still and mindin' things,"[2] Mumbet absorbed what she had heard. She would soon be emboldened to take matters into her own hands. But the time for that would be of her choosing.

Lying awake at night, she turned on her side, worrying about what had become of her husband, who had recently enlisted in the Patriot Army and whose whereabouts were unknown. She couldn't help but be troubled by the irony that he was fighting to protect her master's freedom.

A lone candle lighting the room flickered suddenly as it burned to its base. Mumbet, exhausted from her day's work, closed her eyes and finally slept. Events were slowly but surely moving in her direction.

Northern Bondage

In the years leading up to the Revolutionary War, New Englanders were far more dependent on slave labor than many historians might concede. Africans stripped from the shores of their homeland became artisans, sailors, and sea captains within the region's rum-making and maritime industries.[1] Later, blacks became house servants, soldiers, and field hands, and symbols of success among the lawyers, ministers and merchants who owned them.

Some of the region's most prominent families made their fortunes carrying human cargo, as New England became the nexus of North America's slave trade. Those who opposed slavery were few in number, and their voices were absorbed in a whirlwind of indifference. Mumbet's quest for freedom would become all the more daunting, for she and her advocates would need to confront an established way of life.

Slavery began in New England when a certain Captain William Pierce of Boston traveled to the West Indies in 1638 and traded several Pequot Indians for "salt, cotton, tobacco and negroes . . ."[2] Bay Colony traders later made the longer and far more dangerous journey to Africa in search of slaves. Ultimately, New England seamen brought slaves all the way from the remote island of Madagascar, located near the tip of the East African coast.[3] Massachusetts gave slavery legal sanction in 1641, and laws later evolved to make it "possible for the children of slaves to be legally held in bondage."[4] Slavery was to be limited only to those who were "lawful captives taken in just warres, and such strangers as willfully sell themselves or are sold to us."[5] But the imprecision of the law left a loophole wide enough to let a slave ship sail through it, which is exactly what happened as traders picked up the pace of traffic in human cargo.

If the law was unclear as to who could be seized and held in bondage, it was silent about how long slaves could be kept in captivity. Though laws were never passed to ensure perpetual servitude, owners, by custom, assumed they had such rights. The Puritans of New England looked to the Bible for guidance on this matter. They noted that the ancient Israelites, in accordance with Jewish law, freed their servants after six years. Rhode Island became the only colony in New England to impose a limit on how long blacks were to be enslaved. A statute passed in 1652 fixed the term at ten years. Violators of the law were to be fined forty pounds, a prodigious sum which one would think might act as a deterrent.

Yet the large number of black slaves laboring in Rhode Island was the best evidence that the law was often ignored.[6] Within the colony's Narragansett region there were more than ten plantations, each with more than ten slaves who worked on plots of land that ranged from 1,000 to 5,000 acres.[7] The colony's candle and cosmetics factories, and rum distilleries relied upon a steady stream of slaves. By virtue of its slave farms and its factories, Rhode Island's per capita slave population became the largest in all of New England.[8]

On the eve of the American Revolution, in the diminutive colony of Connecticut, surrounded by Massachusetts to its north, Rhode Island to its east, and New York to its south and to its west, about half of all lawyers, ministers, and public officials owned slaves.[9] Two generations later, no less a luminary of New England's literary past than Nathaniel Hawthorne reflected on the lives led by slaves living in what came to be known as the Constitution State. While traveling to Litchfield, Connecticut, he stopped at a cemetery and recorded in his diary: "In a remote part of the graveyard, remote from the main body of dead people, I noticed a humble, mossy stone, on which I traced out 'To the memory of Julia Africa, servant of Rev.' somebody. There were also the half obliterated traces of other graves, without any monuments, in the vicinity of this one. Doubtless the slaves here mingled their dark clay with the earth."[10]

Before freedom rang "from the prodigious hilltops of New Hampshire" and "from the mighty mountains of New York,"[11] African slaves were sold at auction alongside farm animals and fine china. The *New Hampshire Gazette* alerted the public that at 2:00 PM on Tuesday, the 22nd of April, 1767, in the home of a certain Thomas Beck, "ONE yoke of OXEN, several steers; Cows; Sheep; 1 good Horse; several Calves; with sundry other Things, Wearing apparel &c. ALSO a likely Negro GIRL" were available for purchase.[12]

Animals and slaves were taxed as personal property throughout New England. In an effort to raise revenue, the colony of New Hampshire altered its tax schedule in 1728 to reflect the newly assessed value of each horse and ox at three pounds apiece. For reasons not entirely clear, each hog was taxed at ten pounds. It would be little consolation to "Each Negro, Mulatto and Indian Slave being male" that their value was assessed at twenty pounds.[13]

New England's newspapers listed slaves for sale in much the same way that cars, trucks and toaster ovens appear today. During the sixty-three year period between 1719 and 1781, nearly two-thousand Africans were advertised for sale in the pages of the *Boston Gazette*.[14] Though the newspaper was evidently widely read, those who listed their merchandise made every effort to reach as broad an audience as possible. So it was that for three consecutive weeks, beginning on May 7, 1757, the same ad alerted readers that on the twenty-third of May, in the home of the recently deceased Henry Darrell, a potpourri of worldly possessions would be available for purchase, including:

> Feather Beds, Bedsteads, Chairs, Tables, Desks, Brass and Cooper Ware, 2 Turkey Carpets, a parcel of Ironmongery and Tin Ware, sundry Pieces of Plate, Men's Apparel, and a Collection of Books; also a Negro Man and Woman, and a Horse and Chaise.[15]

An ad printed in the *New England Weekly Journal* in 1732—sure to bring anguish to anyone with a heart that read it—stated simply: "likely negro woman about 19 years and a child of about six months of age to be sold together or apart."[16] Slave owners later began to remove their own names from such ads, for fear that their slaves would learn of their intent to sell them, which, in turn, might—and did—lead many of them to run away.[17]

Just how many slaves lived in Massachusetts by the middle of the eighteenth century will remain forever a matter of conjecture. In 1754, at about the time of Mumbet's birth, William Shirley, the colonial governor of Massachusetts, asked his legislature to tally "the exact number of the negro slaves, both males and females, fifteen years old and upwards."[18] The lawmakers counted 4,489 blacks in what became the first formal census ever taken in the colony.

Nine years later, census takers counted only 2,021 negroes and mulattos, and 370 Indian families, along with 200,000 white citizens in the colony. The reason for the dramatic and mysterious decline in the number of Africans may have been summed up best by Governor Bernard, who noted that "as all returns before mentioned were taken in order to make a rate of taxes . . . they are certainly short of the truth . . . ."[19]

Exactly how far the estimates fell short of the colony's African population will remain unknown, for there are many reasons why the data was flawed. First, the census was unpopular. The colonists felt it was yet another example of British authorities infringing on their rights.[20] Second, the data left out children less than fifteen years of age—a group that must have been quite large, given the low life expectancy of the era. Third, the methods of data gathering were hardly scientific. The colonists assigned to the task had little training, and estimates were based on multipliers applied to militia muster rolls and other lists in a crude attempt to estimate the slave population.[21] Finally, superstition came into play, "as some people believed that sickness or death would follow if the people were counted,"[22] consistent with the Puritan view that King David sinned when he took a census of the Jews. All of these factors led to a dramatic undercounting of the colony's slaves.

If a cursory glance across the region's landscape

revealed just how common was the practice of slavery, then less visible to the naked eye was the impact of the slave trade on its economy. Merchants in the coastal cities of Boston and Newport, Rhode Island, controlled two-thirds of the young nation's slave traffic, making New England the epicenter of the North American slave trade. A sophisticated ecosystem of sailmakers, shipbuilders and insurance companies lent logistical and financial support for the slave trade. Colonial authorities indemnified slave traders from import duties by allowing "drawbacks," if slaves died within the first six weeks to a year after their arrival. [23]

The slave trade was by no means limited to an isolated lot of enterprising merchants. Some of the region's most prominent families benefited from the *transport* of human cargo, as they "made their profits as carriers rather than as exploiters of Negro labor." [24] These included Jonathan Belcher, governor of Massachusetts, and four members of the Wanton family of Rhode Island, who at various times served as governors of the colony.[25]

New England's liquor industry was built on

molasses and sugar imported from the West Indies, where thousands of slaves harvested these crops round the clock for seven days a week. Owners of Newport's thirty rum distilleries tried to keep pace with their Boston neighbors to the north. Slave traders in Boston employed some five thousand sailors, as well as tanners, coopers and sailmakers.[26] The Sugar Act of 1764, an attempt by the mother country to clamp down on the smuggling of molasses and sugar, met severe resistance in the New England colonies. Business owners and employees in the shipbuilding, rum trade and seacoast industries—all of whom depended on a continuous flow of slaves to the colonies—bitterly opposed the law.[27]

While historians generally fault the southern aristocracy for delaying the end of slavery, it is hard to imagine that northern slave traders would have willingly put an end to their own lifeblood. In the twenty-five years after the passage of the Constitution, Rhode Island slave traders almost matched the number of slaves they imported over the prior fifty years. Who knows how many more slaves might have been imported had not the Constitutional Convention banned the slave trade, beginning in 1808.

In New England, slaves were considered property; they could be bought and sold at the discretion of their owners. Slaves were used in place of hard currency to settle debts and were willed to family members. The Reverend John Williams of Deerfield, Massachusetts, left his heirs a library of 349 pamphlets and 190 volumes, as well as "aprons, spoons, six cows, including a 'weak backed' cow . . . the mulatto boy Messek and the black boy Kedar." The two slaves were each appraised at 80 pounds.[28]

Yet, slaves had rights in courts of law, as the Puritans sought to ensure that their slaves "shall have the liberties and Christian usages which the law of G-d established in Israell concerning such persons doth morally require."[29] As a result, slaves testified in court on their own behalf, and on behalf of others. They could also testify against their white masters or other white citizens in courts of law. Suspended between the poles of people and property, blacks made the best of an awkward situation.

Slaves and their advocates looked to the courts as a venue through which to pursue their freedom. Many slaves could and did take their owners to court for physical abuse, for a defect in title of ownership, for mistreatment, for reneging on promises made for their freedom, or for wrongful enslavement.

Jenny Slew, a woman of mixed race origin, was among the first to pursue her freedom in court. The offspring of a white mother and black father, Jenny Slew lived in the coastal village of Ipswich on Boston's North Shore. In 1762, while living as a free woman—or so she thought—Jenny was abducted by a certain John Whipple, who "with force and arms took her the said Jenny, held and kept her in servitude as a slave in his service,"[30] for the next three years. Jenny filed suit against Whipple, seeking damages of 25 pounds. Her case came before the First Inferior Court of Common Pleas in Newburyport, Essex County, in September of 1765. Whipple's attorney argued that "there is no such person in nature as Jenny Slew of Ipswich, aforesaid spinster,"[31] apparently on the basis that "as a married woman she had no identity separate from her husband and therefore could not sue on her own behalf."[32]

The judge ruled against Jenny Slew. But she did not give up so easily. Jenny appealed the verdict on the first Tuesday of November, 1765, before the superior court in nearby Salem, Massachusetts. The case was postponed to the last term by consent. When the case was finally brought before a jury, Jenny gained her freedom, and was awarded four pounds in damages and costs.[33] One of those who witnessed the court's proceedings was John Adams, who noted in his diary on November 5, 1765:

> Attended Court; heard the trial of an action of trespass, brought by a mulatto woman, for damages, for restoring her of her liberty. This is called suing for liberty; the first action that ever I knew of the sort, though I have heard there have been many.[34]

The Jenny Slew case and other freedom suits indicated that jury members could be sympathetic to victims of wrongful enslavement. It was a powerful signal that, in time, had the potential to end an established way of life.

Berkshire Lives

In 1725, a little more than a hundred years after the Pilgrims landed in Plymouth, thirty-five citizens received a land grant from the General Court of Massachusetts. The group agreed to expand the colony's westernmost boundary and gave funds to support a minister and a school and to "extinguish" the claims of the area's Indians. The settlers fulfilled their obligation when they gave the Indians four hundred sixty pounds sterling, thirty quarts of rum, and three barrels of cider.[1] So began the official settlement of what was to become Berkshire County.

The town of Sheffield, located in the southwestern

corner of the settlement, developed a distinct flavor of its own. Its first inhabitants were a curious blend of people: Dutch settlers from the neighboring Hudson Valley region of New York, Puritans who came from the eastern towns of Massachusetts, and Africans who sought freedom and a safe haven from pursuit by their captors who lived in New York.[2]

John Ashley first surveyed the region in the late 1720s, and settled in Sheffield in 1730, several years after graduating from Yale College. Ashley hailed from Hampshire County, what was then the westernmost province of the state. He quickly became Sheffield's leading citizen, and, acting as his father's agent, tended to his sawmill, gristmill, cider mill, and general store. Ashley's fifty cultivated acres made his the largest farm in town, where he worked three teams of horse and oxen. An enterprising pioneer, he brought iron ore by horseback from Salisbury, Connecticut, and soon began his own forging business.[3]

Not long after settling in Sheffield, he married Hannah Hogeboom, the twenty-three-year-old daughter of Pieter and Annette, who were members of the

Dutch Reformed Church, located just over the border which separated Massachusetts from New York. The Ashleys settled into a new home where the wood paneling above the fireplace met the restrictions imposed by Britain's Parliament,[4] for the king insisted that the largest trees be used to form the towering masts of his sailing ships.

A man named John Pynchon marked the earliest record of slave ownership in western Massachusetts when he noted in his journal in the last month of 1687 that "Roco and Sue, my negroes, joined in marriage."[5] Pynchon, a fur trader, had settled along the banks of the Connecticut River in what is now the city of Springfield, Massachusetts. Roco managed to accumulate over sixty acres of land by 1685, yet he remained Pynchon's personal property. Roco gained his freedom ten years later in return for twenty-five 40-gallon barrels of turpentine and twenty-one 40-gallon barrels of "good merchantable Tarr."[6]

"Slaves were by no means an unusual form of property, in former times," Josiah Holland wrote in his epic *History of Western Massachusetts*, published in 1855, just six years before the American Civil War. "There were," according to Holland, "probably a few slaves on every [Massachusetts] plantation, where the wealth of settlers would permit, and negroes were held in bondage in the Connecticut Valley during nearly or quite an entire century of its history."[7]

Slave owners throughout the American colonies had long held the power to break up an immediate family through the purchase and sale of its members. But settlers in western Massachusetts frowned on this behavior. When Sylva, a black slave living in nearby Hampshire County, learned that his owner intended to sell him, he protested with such intensity that his owner decided against it.[8] A minister in Westfield, familiar with the incident, wrote that "Masters of Negroes ought to be men of great humanity. They have an arbitrary power, may correct them at pleasure, may separate them from their children, may send them out of the Country."[9] Not everyone was sensitive to the minister's sentiments, for in 1746, at around the time of Mumbet's birth, the *Boston Evening Post* noted it was "very surprising that a local Negro couple should be so devoted to one another as to commit suicide upon learning that the woman would be sold into the country."[10]

John Ashley owned three black men, John, Zack, and Harry, who lived in a separate section of his home. The men may have been purchased in slave markets in Hartford, Connecticut, some forty miles to the southeast of Sheffield, or in Albany, a city some forty miles to its west, where "slaves were said to be treated more cruelly than in any other Northern city."[11]

Into the home of John Ashley, Mumbet and her sister Lizzie arrived as slaves sometime in their childhood. Though Mumbet would develop a reputation as "a woman who was all humbleness on the surface but iron underneath,"[12] the most basic aspects of her ancestry remain a mystery, including her birth date, family heritage, and the African tribe of her origin. A silk shawl once owned by her father and a short gown that belonged to her mother were Mumbet's only heirlooms.

It is not entirely clear how the Ashleys came to

own Bett and her sister. One theory suggests Mumbet and Lizzie became Hannah Ashley's property upon the death of her father in 1758. The theory finds support in the tenth paragraph of Pieter Hogeboom's will, where he wrote:

> I bequeath to all my children . . . all my negroes and negresses, big and little, young and old, all my horses and cattle and furthermore all my movable goods from the largest to the smallest that may be found after my death, to each his just tenth part.[13]

While Hannah is named as one of her father's ten beneficiaries, the names of his slaves are omitted, leading us to wonder whether Mumbet and her sister really were inherited by Hannah Ashley, or came to the Ashley household by some other means. The story persists, due in part to local legend. Electa Jones, in her town history of Stockbridge, notes that Bett and her sister were carried to Sheffield across the snowcapped hills of Claverack "on the bottom of a sleigh, covered by straw."[14]

Another possibility, supported by an Ashley descendent, is that Mumbet and her sister were purchased at the Albany slave market.[15] There we can imagine the two standing on an auctioneer's block, their destiny determined by the highest bidder. The decision to sell them together may have been inspired by someone with a heart. Could it have been Bett who insisted on their remaining together? Or might it have been that John Ashley and his wife took pity on the two and agreed to purchase them? We will never know. The only certainty is that Mumbet and her sister Lizzie became Hannah Ashley's personal property.

Mumbet and Lizzie served at the personal whim of their master and mistress, where they performed physical labor, as well as the many maidservant tasks involved in helping to raise four children. All indications are that Mumbet became an indispensable servant to Hannah Ashley, who was the most powerful woman in town. There, at her beck and call, Mumbet performed her duties with personal dignity, and soon became well known throughout the town for her talent, wit, and fortitude.

A small water color painting on ivory survives of

Mumbet. Measuring a mere 2" x 3", it provides an image of how she looked in her later years. One is drawn immediately to her soft round features. Her eyes contain a certain liveliness, and convey a sense that she wants those who gaze upon her to know she is a free woman. In her eyes I detect sadness, stemming from the sacrifices she made in her life. Mumbet's shoulders are broad and muscular, an indication of her—or her ancestors'—ability to survive a brutal process of Darwinian selection, for only the fittest endured the middle passage from Africa to America.

We do not know when Mumbet married, the name of her husband, or many details about the couple's child. But it is not surprising that we do not know these details, for in most cases records of civil ceremonies of marriage and birth were not maintained for the colony's black citizens.

There is reason to believe that John Ashley and Hannah Hogeboom Ashley differed in their views about slavery, and this may have been a source of tension between the two as they discussed how to treat the slaves living with them.[16] The differences were understandable, given the varying geographies, social customs, laws, and religions that split them. For starters, the colony of New York, in which Hannah Hogeboom grew up, had the largest slave population of any northern colony. New York had more black slaves than Georgia, and two of every five white households owned slaves in Manhattan in the 1760s.[17] Black slaves living in New York city comprised one-third of its labor force at the outset of the American Revolution.[18]

Growing up in the village of Claverack, New York, near Albany, Hannah Hogeboom was exposed at an early age to the savagery of slavery. New York imposed severe penalties on slaves who violated the law. Slaves traveling alone within a forty-mile radius of Albany could be put to death, in keeping with a law passed in 1705.[19] Close to Claverack, slave traders in the city of Albany operated two slave markets. A census taken in 1790 in Old Kinderhook, New York, of which Claverack was a part, indicates that slaves accounted for nearly 15 percent of the population.

The town historian noted that "Slaves were held here at a very early period and in increasing numbers, and thus continued to be until slavery ceased," which occurred on July 4, 1827, more than 50 years after the Declaration of Independence.[20] As a child growing up in Claverack, Hannah Hogeboom was therefore surrounded by slaves, and grew up with many families who owned them. By contrast, there were no slave markets in the Berkshires, where, from its earliest times, free and enslaved blacks had lived side by side.

Catharine Maria Sedgwick—the early American novelist and daughter of the man who would one day help Mumbet pursue her freedom—provides insight into her character and ability to stand up, when necessary, to her callow mistress. Her essay, "Slavery in New England," published in 1853, only a year after Harriett Beecher Stowe's *Uncle Tom's Cabin* reached enraptured readers, captures the true spirit of Mumbet. The story, as told by Mumbet to a young Catharine, begins:

> It was in May . . . just at the time of the apple

> blossoms; I was wetting the bleaching linen, when a smallish girl came in to the gate, and up the lane, and straight to me, and said, without raising her eyes, "Where is your master? I must speak with him." I told her that my master was absent, that he would come home before night.[21]

The girl who came to the Ashley's home that evening was a "gal in trouble," which in the parlance of the times could have only a single meaning. Evidently this was not the first time the judge had been approached for advice in such matters, an indication of his reputation for fairness and a sympathetic nature.

Mumbet continued:

> I never saw one like this. The blood seemed to have stopped in her veins; her face and neck were all in blotches of red and white. She had bitten her lip through; her voice was hoarse and husky, and her eyelids seemed to settle down as if she could never raise them again.[22]

Bett invited the timid girl to wait in a bedroom in the house until John Ashley returned home later that evening. When Hannah Ashley saw the child, she confronted Bett. Bett told her of the girl's desire to meet privately with the judge. Angered by Bett's solidarity with the stranger in their midst, Hannah erupted into one of her tantrums, and as Bett recalled, "there was no foul thing she didn't call the child."

But Bett was not one to back down, especially when she knew she was right. "Sit still, child," she advised the girl. When Hannah again tried to drive her from the house by intimidating Bett, the girl became terrified. But Bett sensed a certain weakness on the part of her mistress. As she explained to Catharine Sedgwick, "When I set my foot down, I kept it down."[23]

Later that evening, in the dim light of his study, John Ashley listened to the girl's story. He was visibly shaken when he sat down and saw her clearly for the first time. "If ever there was a pitiful look," according to Bett, "it was that look of master's. I can see it yet." Then the girl swore before the judge that every word she was about to tell was the truth.

We are left only to imagine the horrible cruelty the girl had received at the hands of her father, as she confided her story to the judge.

The perpetrator of the crime was later brought before John Ashley, and forced to confront his daughter. Mumbet recalled that when the father entered the room, "every hair stood stiff and upright on his head."

The father was sent east to Hampshire County for a criminal trial, but while awaiting his fate, the girl was abducted by her father's friends, who sought to prevent her testimony at trial. The girl was sent into exile, so that she would be safe from any attempt by her father to dole out his definition of country justice. The father was ultimately condemned. The girl, we are told, died a short time later. It would not be the last time Mumbet would speak up in the face of injustice.

* * *

As a judge, and the largest land and slave owner of the town of Sheffield, John Ashley was among the area's most influential citizens. He would soon be among those who would play a leading role as the people of Berkshire were drawn into the conflict between the king and his colonies.

John Ashley, along with other leading Berkshire citizens, protested to Parliament in 1768 that it had no right to tax them without, in return, providing a say in domestic matters. The British secretary of state, Lord Hillsborough, confronted the colonists and insisted that they reverse their stance. The colonial governor, Bernard, received instructions to implement his decree. Ninety-two Massachusetts men in the general assembly remained opposed to Parliament, but seventeen relented in the face of intimidation by the colonial officials.[24] Governor Bernard dissolved the assembly in an act of retribution.

John Ashley was one of six Berkshire County men who backed down from the original letter. He became known as a "rescinder," or one of the "obnoxious 17," who were later scorned by Patriots throughout the colony.[25] It would not be the last time John Ashley would back down in the face of overwhelming pressure.

Ashley, acting as the sole representative for several towns, did not anticipate the backlash unleashed by his vote. Great Barrington's residents rebuked

Ashley for his decision to back down, an action which "was, and still is, repugnant to the sense and opinion of the inhabitants of this town."[26] Ashley's role as a "rescinder" long lingered in the memory of Great Barrington.

Ashley reemerged later as a member of the Patriot camp, as the road to revolution intensified in the early 1770s. He headed a town committee that wrote a series of grievances designed to address the increasingly diminutive domestic role the colonies were asked to assume by the British crown. A group of town leaders began to gather in his home to discuss measures that might be taken to protest against the royal government.

Though they could not read or write, Mumbet and her sister Lizzie listened to the men discuss how they planned to wrestle their rights away from a king who lived across the sea. Bett thought about what it might be like to be free. She wondered whether the men gathered in the parlor sensed the paradox of their plans to gain their freedom, while she and others in the town remained enslaved.

One of those who attended the sessions was Theodore Sedgwick, a twenty-seven year old attorney. Mumbet must have noted Sedgwick's passion for the Patriot cause, and wondered whether he would agree that the liberty they sought for themselves ought to include her as well. Mumbet must have made a favorable impression on the young attorney with a deep-seated ambition to advance his own career. Neither one realized at the time just how much their future would depend upon the other.

Born outside the town of Hartford, Connecticut, Theodore Sedgwick and his family moved to Cornwall, Connecticut, when he was barely two years old in 1748. Tragedy struck the Sedgwick household when his father Benjamin died from a sudden stroke in early February of 1757, at the age of 41. The unexpected timing of his death is revealed on his tombstone, which reads:

> In an Instant He is Call'd
> Eternity to View,
> No time to regulate his house,
> Or bid his friends adieu.[27]

Benjamin's death left his wife, Ann, their ten-year-old son, Theodore, and his older brother, John, in a precarious position. John became a tavern keeper and farmer, and had a strong hand in raising his younger brother, as well as their siblings. As a child, Theodore Sedgwick, was, according to his sole biographer, Richard Welch, "respected by his contemporaries as a fair swimmer and a persistent, if somewhat clumsy, skater."[28]

Two images survive to give us an impression of Theodore Sedgwick. In one, an engraving, the eyes are soft and kind, as Theodore Sedgwick bears a benevolent, almost mischievous look on his face. In the second, an oil painting, Sedgwick has an imperial, almost regal appearance, befitting his future role as the legislative leader of the Federalist Party.

Sedgwick's family heritage must have made him think more than twice about the need to break away from Britain. His great-grandfather, Robert Sedgwick, was born in England in 1613. He settled in Charlestown, Massachusetts in 1636, and the next year created a "commodious brewry."[29] Robert

Sedgwick's ambition animated him to achieve much success at an early age, as he became a captain at the age of 27 in the military company of Massachusetts. Later, he, along with six others, was given a monopoly on the colony's Indian trade for a period of twenty-one years.[30] Robert Sedgwick would later pursue the French enemies of the British in Nova Scotia, situated several hundred miles to the north and the east of Boston. Sedgwick's success in battle drew the praise of Oliver Cromwell (1599–1658), the British lord protector. He later sent Robert to fight the Dutch in a military conquest on the island of Barbados. There, as disease set in, and his enemies surrounded him, Robert Sedgwick perished.

Robert Sedgwick's great-grandson, Theodore, entered Yale College at the age of 15 in the winter of 1761–1762, at a time when less than one percent of the Colonial population pursued higher education. Theodore Sedgwick was determined to make his mark on the world around him, though not in quite the same way as his illustrious ancestor. At Yale, matters got off to an inauspicious start, as Sedgwick became involved in a series of student uprisings protesting, among other things, the passage of the Stamp Act in 1765. Other students objected to a series of tuition hikes. All of this contributed to the unpopular tenure of Thomas Clap, president of the college. His regime ended abruptly when students, in a fit of fury, tore down and ran away with the steel fence that surrounded his home.[31] Although it remains a mystery as to why Theodore Sedgwick, late in the course of his senior year, was abruptly dismissed from Yale, his participation in unspecified "boyish gaieties"[32] leaves one to infer that he may have been a ringleader in the prank against the college president.

Sedgwick was later reinstated at Yale, likely as an act of clemency on the part of college administrators, who may have agreed with Sedgwick's daughter who later noted that Clap was a "compound of pedagogue and granny."[33] Theodore began to study theology, with an eye toward the ministry. This may have been less an act of repentance for his youthful folly, than due to the fact that nearly half of Yale's students at the time prepared for the pulpit.

Divinity school did not sit well with Theodore Sedgwick. Upon further reflection, he decided to settle in the Berkshire town of Great Barrington, where he studied law under Mark Hopkins, a relative, and younger brother of the famed Protestant theologian. Hopkins helped him prepare for admission to the Massachusetts Bar the next year, in 1766. After a year of waiting patiently for the townspeople to discover his legal acumen, he moved his office four miles south to Sheffield in search of greener pastures.[34]

The next year, at the age of 22, he married Elizabeth Mason, the daughter of Deacon Jeremiah Mason. Theodore Sedgwick soon became part of the town's elite, and owned twenty-three acres of land and at least one black house servant, named Caesar.[35] Then, only a month before Elizabeth was to give birth to their first child, tragedy struck when she died of the dreaded smallpox.[36] His grief was compounded by the fact that, according to family tradition, he may have transmitted the disease to her, while she was combing his long hair, although he had been certified by a local physician as noninfectious.

Sedgwick faced a bout of depression from which he may never have fully recovered. In an effort to block the pain, he threw himself headlong into political matters. John Ashley, who at the time was fifty-eight years old, and old enough to be Sedgwick's father, soon became a friend, colleague, and mentor. Ashley may have exerted a paternal influence over Sedgwick, who was searching for a mentor in a world he scarcely knew.

Together, they became a leading force in creating what came to be known as the *Sheffield Resolves*, a landmark document written in 1773, in which eleven of the town elders wrote:

> RESOLVED, That mankind in a state of nature are equal, free, and independent of each other, and have a right to the undisturbed enjoyment of their lives, their liberty and property.
>
> RESOLVED, That the great end of political society is to secure in a more effectual manner those rights and privileges wherewith G-d and nature have made us free.[37]

From their precarious position alongside the stair

banister of Ashley's home, Bett and Lizzie strained to listen to the men discuss the King's transgressions. Attuned to the idea of freedom, Bett wondered whether the document might apply to them.

The next year, some of Sheffield's citizens submitted a motion at a town meeting in which they protested against "the inhuman practice of inslaving our fellow creatures, the natives of Africa." [38] Bett may have heard the rumor about the motion passed in town on one of her trips to the general store. She wondered who had spoken up on her behalf, and on behalf of her fellow townspeople who remained enslaved.

Sometime later she learned that the motion had been deferred, since the idea was being pursued by the colony's legislature.[39] In the news she sensed a silver lining: at least some of her fellow citizens had stepped forward on her behalf. As she turned south from the town's general store, and made her way down the main street to return home, she looked east to a large open field, where the Berkshire hills rose majestically in the distance. She smiled to herself as she walked a now familiar path with a newfound feeling of hope.

Awakening

As the colonies collided on a course of rebellion against the British government, some New Englanders began to see the link between slave ownership and the slave trade. There were others who perceived the injustice of slavery to be incompatible with the struggle for American independence. In 1765, the year of the infamous Stamp Act, a representative from Worcester, a town located some eighty miles to the east of Sheffield, was told to "use his influence to obtain a law to put an end to that unchristian and impolitic practice of making slaves of the human species."[1] Two years later, Worcester citizens introduced a bill calling for an end to "the unwarrantable and unlawful Practice or Custom of inslaving Mankind in this Province, and the importation of slaves into the same."[2] The seeds of abolition began to spread, but its foundation remained tenuous.

Precious few of the region's citizens spoke out against the vicious nature of the slave trade. One who did was Nathaniel Appleton, a candle maker and the son of a prominent Puritan minister.[3] In his *Considerations on Slavery*, published in 1767, Appleton exposed in print the horrors of the slave trade, writing:

> Oh! Methinks I hear their screeches, rending the very heavens, when these horrid scenes take place! The unhappy healthy are immediately hand-tied, and then two and two are yoked by their necks like horses for shipping, and drove in herds by their masters to the sea-coast, and stow'd in the hold of a vessel.[4]

Appleton pointed out the hypocrisy of "an American-Captain, trading upon the Guinea Coast for slaves," who would "open his mouth and plead for liberty, and his natural rights." Appleton went on to argue that it would be far better if "while we are preventing the chains being put upon us, we are knocking them off from those who already have them on . . ."[5]

Just two years before the outbreak of the War of Independence, four black men circulated a leaflet calling for freedom with a letter that began: "We expect great things from men who have made such a noble stand against the designs of their fellow-men to enslave them."[6] Thomas Hutchinson, the royal governor of Massachusetts, preoccupied with other matters, told the men that he could not help them.

Blacks petitioned the newly appointed British governor Thomas Gage in more pointed language the next year, hoping his response might be different. In their letter dated May 25, 1774, they wrote:

> We were unjustly dragged by the cruel hand of power from our dearest friends and Sum of us stolen from the bosoms of our tender Parents and from a Populous Pleasant and plentiful Country and Brought hither to be made slaves for Life in a Christian land.[7]

Progress would be postponed once more as King and colonists continued down the path toward Revolution.

Shots fired at Lexington and Concord echoed to the east and to the west, signaling the start of the colonial rebellion in April of 1775. Berkshire County heard the call, sending many of her sons to join the American Army gathering in Cambridge, a village one hundred miles to the east of Sheffield.

The spring of 1775 was a particularly rough period for Mumbet as she watched over her frail sister, Lizzie, while, at the same time, she worried for her husband's safety. He may have been among the first to enlist in the American army. At least three black men from Sheffield—James Storm, Humphrey Hubbard, and "Guy"—served in the War of Independence.[8] Could this third man, whose last name was not identified, have been the husband of Mumbet? Though we do not know which battles he fought in, we do know that Mumbet's husband never returned from the war. It is likely she never learned of his fate.

As the war wore on, there were those who sought to

keep the topic of slavery near the top of the national agenda. Samuel Hopkins, once a slave owner, underwent a conversion of sorts midway through his career. After serving for a time as a minister in the Berkshire village of Great Barrington, he left, and accepted an appointment as minister for a congregation in Newport, Rhode Island. Somewhere along the way, he concluded that slavery was inconsistent with his Puritan faith. He became an outspoken critic and opponent of slavery and the slave trade. His outspokenness was all the more courageous since many of the members of his congregation in Newport bought, sold, and transported Africans.

In early 1776, about a year after the battles of Lexington and Concord, and only a few months before the signing of the Declaration of Independence, Hopkins published *A Dialogue Concerning the Slavery of the Africans*, a 72-page book dedicated to the honorable members of the U.S. Congress. Written against the backdrop of an outbreak of illegal seizure of black slaves living in New York, Hopkins presented his view as a debate between an advocate of slavery and an opponent. Hopkins exposed the hypocrisy of defending slavery while pursuing freedom from the British. For Hopkins, the American Revolution would always lack a moral foundation for as long as slavery existed. Unfortunately, Hopkins's words were not acted upon.

Closer to Mumbet's home, Massachusetts legislators gathered in the autumn of 1777 to begin debate over a constitution for the state. One of the key issues was whether blacks and Indians should be eligible to vote. Newspaper editorials captured the intensity of the debate:

> Would it not be ridiculous, inconsistent and unjust, to exclude freemen from voting for representatives and senators, though otherwise qualified, because their skins are black, tawny or reddish? Why not disqualified for being long nosed, short-faced, or higher or lower than five feet nine? [9]

Ultimately, lawmakers settled on a constitution for the state of Massachusetts. Most relevant to our story is Article V, which allowed "every male inhabitant of any town in this State, being free, and twenty-one years of age," to vote—"excepting Negroes, Indians and molattoes."[10]

A certain Dr. Gordon, who served as chaplain to both houses of the legislature, was one of the few to speak out against the provision:

> The complexion of the 5th Article is blacker than that of any African; and if not altered, will be an everlasting reproach upon the present inhabitants; and evidence to the world, that they mean their own rights only, and not those of mankind, in their cry for liberty.[11]

Gordon went on to chide the lawmakers over who else might be excluded from voting under the new law:

> As to Molattoes they should have been defined. We should have been told, whether it intended the offspring of a white and Negro, or also of a white and Indian; and whether the immediate offspring alone, or any of their remote descendants . . .[12]

Gordon was later dismissed from his office, due in part to his having "rashly reflected upon the General Court.[3] Several towns weighed in on the subject, including Westminster, whose members roundly rejected the constitution, based on Article V, as did its neighbor Sutton, whose citizens noted "the already accumulated Load of guilt lying upon the Land in Supporting the Slave Trade . . . ." By a nearly five to one vote, the constitution of 1778 was rejected.[14]

Two years later, lawmakers made some progress in search of a new constitution, which included a clause, drafted by John Adams, which held that "All men are born free and equal, and have certain natural, essential and unalienable rights; among which may be reckoned the right of enjoying, and defending their lives and liberties; that of acquiring, possessing, and protecting property; in fine, that of seeking and obtaining their safety and happiness."[15] Though this constitution stopped short of providing general equality for the colony's black and Indian citizens, some saw potential in its broad-based declaration.

* * *

On a cold afternoon in late winter, Bett and her sister Lizzie were busy baking bread for their owners.[16] It was a day like many others, as Lizzie hoped the wheat cakes she placed in the oven would find favor with their mistress. The product of her labor this afternoon seemed particularly enticing to her, though she had often prepared it in much the same way before.

Lizzie used the end pieces from the bread to make her afternoon snack, thinking it would not be missed by her mistress. Emerging from the living room in a particularly foul mood, Madame Ashley entered the kitchen. Panning around the warm, bread-scented room, her eyes were drawn to Bett's meek younger sister, curled up in a corner, peacefully enjoying the fruits of her labor.

Ashley seized the kitchen shovel lying beside the oven, and, raising it above her head, threatened Lizzie, scolding her for the brazen late-afternoon enjoyment. Hearing the commotion from the next room, Bett quickly wheeled into motion, sensing that once again she would need to restrain her untamable owner.

As she entered the kitchen, Bett took in an all-too-familiar scene: a ranting mistress taking out her frustrations on a weak slave. But somehow something was different this time. Perhaps it was the venom emanating from Ashley and the smoldering embers of the shovel falling to the floor. Maybe it was the feeling that this situation never should have come to be, nor be repeated in the future. Bett realized there was only one action to take.

As she moved to shield her sister from their raging mistress, the shovel struck Bett's arm. She groaned in agony as the shovel came crashing to the floor. A gasping mistress, surprised by what her cruelty had wrought, watched for a moment as the bulbous blotch on Bett's black skin turned to purple. Lizzie, still seated on the ground, cried out in sympathy for her sister.

Bett, angry and still writhing from the blow to her arm, stormed from the house. As she tried to block out the sudden throbbing sensation, her rage gave way to a feeling of defiance that had long fermented inside her.

The sun set over a wide swath of evergreen trees, and the white snow began to turn a grayish hue. The crimson sky overhead signaled that the day had drawn to a close. Given the changing world around her, Mumbet realized it might no longer be necessary to endure the cruelty of her unstable mistress. Other slaves had taken action to change their lot in life. Why couldn't she? Who might help her in her quest for freedom? Then she had a thought: *what about Theodore Sedgwick?*

At the outbreak of the War of Independence, Theodore Sedgwick volunteered for service in the ill-fated Canadian campaign, one of the war's most brutal, during which the Patriot general John Thomas and several hundred soldiers died of the dreaded smallpox. The living were then forced to retreat in the face of British and Canadian pursuit along the northern frontier.

Aaron Burr, a Patriot who participated in Benedict Arnold's mission to Quebec, had tried to persuade Sedgwick to become a military aid to General Israel Putnam, a post Burr believed would be "more adequate to his abilities."[17] With Burr's assistance, Sedgwick became commissioner of supply for the Northern Department in the Continental Army.

Sedgwick operated, in effect, a small trading post, where he would buy food and supplies from local proprietors, and sell the goods at slight mark-up to the army. His success in this post would later cause George Washington to consider Sedgwick as a candidate for secretary of the treasury.

Coming home from the war in 1777, Sedgwick developed a thriving law practice and became one of the wealthiest citizens of Berkshire County. A sign of Sedgwick's rising status in the community was his ownership of several slaves. On the first of July, 1777, Sedgwick bought Ton, a black woman, and a girl from a man named John Fellows.[18] Sedgwick's grandson would later speculate that his grandfather's decision "was undoubtedly done from humane motives, and probably to save the 'chattels' from a hard taskmaster."[19]

In 1780, Theodore Sedgwick was elected Sheffield's representative to the newly formed Massachusetts House of Representatives, following the passage of the state's constitution, another indication that his star was on the rise.

Bett sensed that Sedgwick was an open-minded, if ambitious, attorney. Even if he had owned slaves, she believed he would give her a fair hearing. But, for now, Bett took no action. Instead she made sure that Madame Ashley's friends became familiar with her mistress' true character. When guests visited the Ashley house that winter, Bett made sure her lacerated arm was exposed for all to see. When they asked how she had hurt herself, she simply referred them to Mistress Ashley for her account of the story. Bett's behavior increased support for her cause, as she sent her mistress the message that her actions were unacceptable. In describing the story, Catharine Sedgwick wondered aloud, "who was the master and who was the slave?"[20]

As Bett mulled over her situation, a hundred miles to the east a slave-for-sale advertisement ran in Boston's *Continental Journal* on the first of March, 1781:

> To be SOLD, an extraordinary likely Negro WENCH, 17 years old, she can be warranted to be strong, healthy and good-natured, has no notion of Freedom, has been always used to a Farmer's

> Kitchen and dairy, and is not known to have any failing, but being with Child, which is the cause of her being sold.[21]

This was Mumbet's world. She, on the other hand, was becoming attuned to freedom. And she wasn't the only one: Berkshire County was already gaining a reputation as a safe haven for free blacks. This was particularly galling to a certain Reuben Hopkins, who placed an ad in the *Connecticut Courant* in March of 1779, offering a twenty dollar reward for his "Negro wench named Zil," who, small for her age, "pretends she is free" and the "last she has been heard of she was going to Lenox,"[22] a couple of towns to the north of Sheffield.

When Massachusetts ratified its state constitution, word spread of the guarantee that all men are created free and equal. In keeping with what has become a longstanding New England tradition of reading aloud important pronouncements in public places, Mumbet traveled the distance from the Ashley house to the Congregational Church, to be among the first to hear the Constitution read from atop the building's stone steps.

As Bett stood listening, her mind reached back in time to the meetings held in John Ashley's home, where the Sheffield Resolves were written. The words she heard today were strikingly similar. As she glanced to her left and to her right, she noticed several fellow slaves and some free blacks of Sheffield. She also saw the farmers of Berkshire, many of whom she knew were sympathetic to her plight. Bett shook her head. It just didn't make sense to her that she should be among those enslaved. Nor did it seem right that any person should be the property of another if the words she heard were as self-evident as they seemed.

Smoke rose from the stone chimney of the home across the way, which belonged to Theodore Sedgwick. Bett was comforted by the familiar scent of burning wood. She watched a steady stream of gray smoke bellow forth in the open air until it was preyed upon by the wind. She closed her eyes and took in a deep breath. The crisp autumn air flowed into her nostrils and into her lungs, making her feel even more hungry for the freedom she knew she deserved. As Bett began to focus on the four-mile trek back to the Ashley house, she paused for a moment when a sudden gust of wind gathered a pile of leaves, some gold, some blazing red, some a light brown, into a swirling ball. She paused in her tracks, mesmerized by the leaves as they danced before her eyes.

Why not pay a visit to Theodore Sedgwick, she thought, the man she knew had played such a central role in writing the Sheffield Resolves and who, she may not have known, played a role in writing the Constitution she had just heard.

Mumbet walked across the street to the classic story-and-a-half New England farmhouse that was Theodore Sedgwick's home. How could she express herself in a way that would make sense to him? She felt a sudden sensation of self-doubt, a pang of anxiety in her stomach, thinking he might downplay the notion that the words she had just heard applied to her.

Bett was greeted at the door by Pamela Sedgwick,

Theodore's wife, who cast a curious eye on her unexpected visitor. As Bett began to speak, Pamela recognized her smile and quickly motioned her through the front door with a flapping, welcoming hand. Bett gladly accepted the mug of hot cider Pamela carried from the kitchen. Closing her eyes for a moment, she breathed in the sweet scent of cinnamon. Her hand began to thaw against the hot ceramic cup she grasped ever more tightly. She began to sense the warmth of the home she had just entered, and wondered for a moment what it would be like to live there.

Bett gazed at the fireplace where two logs burned, one atop the other. The log on the bottom crackled suddenly, sending forth a bursting flame. It startled Bett. She straightened up in her chair, waiting anxiously for Sedgwick's arrival.

When Theodore Sedgwick entered the room, Bett rose to greet him. His smile signaled that the short speech she prepared would not be as difficult to deliver as she had feared. They exchanged pleasantries, as they faced one another, seated before the fire. According to tradition, Bett asked the question that would become the basis for her freedom suit.[23] "I heard the words read on the steps of the town hall about all men being free and equal. I am not a dumb critter, won't the law give me my freedom?"

Sedgwick smiled, visibly moved by her plea. He slipped back into his chair, and folding his hands below his chin, gazed straight into Bett's eyes. His silence caused Bett to stir in her seat. Sedgwick leaned forward, and with both hands on the arms of his chair, let out a heavy sigh. She was relieved that the ally she hoped would be on her side really was.

Sedgwick, I suspect, had already taken a liking to Bett, and her humble yet outspoken manner. But before he could help her, he would have to part ways with John Ashley, his friend, mentor, and client.

Somewhere along the way, Sedgwick had changed his mind about slavery. It may have been a personal awakening that caused him to realize no matter how well-treated were his servants, they no longer should be held in captivity. The switch for Sedgwick was a simple one. His servants would receive payment for their work. Theodore Sedgwick, Puritan, maverick, successful lawyer, and possessed of a vaulting ambition to do the right thing, was eager to seize the chance to play a defining role in what was soon to become the end of an era and the beginning of a new one.

Trial

Theodore Sedgwick soon realized that winning Mumbet's freedom would be no simple task. By law, and through custom and tradition, slavery had existed in Massachusetts for over a hundred years. Sedgwick knew, moreover, that he would be taking on John Ashley, a former judge, and the most powerful citizen of Sheffield. It was certain that he would choose experienced counsel to help him.

Though slaves could—and did—bring suit against their owners for excessive violence, a defect in title, or improper seizure, there was no precedent for a slave suing her master on the principal of general equality.

Given this peculiar paradox of slaves as people and property, it would take a creative legal mind to enable Bett to gain her freedom.

Though Theodore Sedgwick had no reason to doubt his own expertise, he turned to Tapping Reeve, a legal scholar who lived in Litchfield, Connecticut. Sedgwick probably met Reeve through Aaron Burr, Reeve's brother-in-law, and a friend of Sedgwick's. Mumbet was fortunate that Reeve arrived on the scene. Reeve loved teaching, he loved the law; and, most importantly, he loved to win. Together, they would develop a legal strategy to free Mumbet.

Tapping Reeve grew up on Long Island, in New York. His father, Abner, a Presbyterian minister, preached his last sermon in Brattleboro Vermont at the age of eighty-five.[1] The younger Reeve enrolled in the College of New Jersey, later renamed Princeton, in the same year that his mother Deborah Tapping passed away. Aggrieved by the loss of his mother and determined to honor her memory, he graduated first in his college class.

Reeve met his future wife when he was hired to

tutor Sally and Aaron Burr, the children of the Reverend Aaron Burr, who died while serving as the second president of Princeton. Sally and Aaron were also the grandchildren of Jonathan Edwards, the famed New Light theologian, who was selected to succeed their father as president of the college. Jonathan Edwards and his daughter succumbed to an epidemic of smallpox which plagued the village of Princeton, leaving Aaron and Sally orphaned at an early age.

Reeve evidently took a strong liking to Sally Burr, for they were married in 1773 when she was eighteen. Tapping Reeve quickly acquired a reputation as a talented attorney. He began teaching law from a bedroom in his home to supplement his income during the Revolutionary War. A few years later, he founded the first law school in America, where he created a mock courtroom in which students could test their debating skills. In 1780, only a year before Mumbet's freedom suit, Sally Reeve bore the couple's first and only child. He added a wing to his home so that she, in poor health, would not be forced to climb the stairs.

Tapping Reeve would later be described by his friend, the Reverend Lyman Beecher, as having "a beaming expression of intelligence and benevolence, while his soft gray hair fell in silver tresses to his shoulders in a style peculiar to himself."[2] Reeve's voice "was singular, having failed from some unknown cause, so that he always spoke in a whisper, and yet so distinctly that a hundred students at once could take notes as he delivered his law lectures."[3] Years later, a local Connecticut newspaper, reporting on a meeting he attended, wrote: "It is certain that Judge Reeve opened his mouth . . . and some say that they heard him speak."[4]

Mumbet was fortunate to tap into the advice of Tapping Reeve for another reason: Reeve was an early advocate of woman's legal rights, and he would later become famous for his *Law of Barron and Femme,* which became a critical contribution to helping women achieve legal status before the law.

One of the first challenges facing the team was whether any woman—black or white—could file a suit on her own, and be recognized in a court of law. Sedgwick and Reeve wanted to be sure their suit would not be dismissed on mere procedural grounds. Mumbet may have suggested the remedy: she knew of another black slave named Brom who was owned by John Ashley's son. Sedgwick and Reeve added him as a co-plaintiff to the suit. Perhaps they reasoned that a man and woman acting together would have a better chance of gaining their freedom than a woman acting alone. This leads us to speculate whether there may have been a closer relationship between Brom and Bett. The court record, however, clearly identifies Bett as a "spinster" and Brom as a "laborer." Adding Brom had another benefit, for it enabled the team to add John Ashley's son as a codefendant, thus ensuring that there would be no excuse to delay the trial in the event that the senior Ashley, who at the time was 71 years of age, could not appear before the court.

Mumbet was not the first slave of John Ashley's to file a suit against him in search of freedom. Attorneys for Zack Mullen, another slave of John Ashley's, had filed a suit on the basis of "trespass," a legal term which implied physical harm had been done to him.

For unknown reasons, Mullen's case had been postponed several times.[5] Perhaps Bett and Brom would benefit from the knowledge that other slaves of John Ashley had been mistreated. Ashley, a lawyer and recently retired judge, turned to two noted attorneys for assistance: one was David Noble, a citizen of Lanesboro, who would, like Sedgwick, become one of the first trustees of Williams College. The other was John Canfield of Sharon, a town located to the south of Berkshire county, just over the Connecticut border.

This would clearly have been considered an important trial. The presence of the region's most distinguished legal minds, the postponement of the Zach Mullen trial, and the timing of the trial—less than a year after the passage of the state's constitution—was evidence that Reeve and Sedgwick intended to test the document's "free and equal" clause.[6]

Brom and Bett vs. J. Ashley, Esq. commenced in May of 1781 when Sedgwick and Reeve issued a *writ of replevin*, a civil procedure under English common law to recover improperly gained property. The court clerk delivered the writ to John Ashley and his son, who were warned that unless Brom and Bett "were taken by our special command, or by the command of our Chief Justice, or for Homicide, or for any other just cause . . . or that you should signify to us the cause"[7] they must be delivered to the court.

John Ashley, however, "did not permit a delivery of the aforesaid Brom and Bett to be made because he asserted that the said Brom and Bett were his Servants for Life, thereby claiming a right of servitude . . ."[8] The Ashleys refused to comply with several orders issued by the court. However, they finally relented, and the case was scheduled for August 21, some three months after the court order was issued.

Theodore Sedgwick could not have been more pleased by the choice of venue, the County Court of Common Pleas, just a few miles north of Sheffield in the town of Great Barrington. Court records leading up to the trial reveal that Sedgwick had been a frequent visitor to the court throughout the year. He was very much a known quantity, and had won many cases there. Furthermore, he was related to Mark Hopkins, one of Great Barrington's favorite sons, who had died in the Revolutionary War. Sedgwick risked his own life in an attempt to save Hopkins during the war. Bett, Brom, Sedgwick and Reeve also stood to benefit from the fact that many within Great Barrington recalled Ashley's recanting in the face of British authorities in the critical period before the Revolution. Sedgwick and Reeve hoped the judge and jurors might be less than sympathetic to the Ashleys, who controlled much of the neighboring town.

But it would be wrong for Sedgwick and Reeve to be overconfident, for they would have to contend with the long-standing precedent of slave ownership, as well as persuade the judge, William Whiting. Born in Bozrah, Connecticut, Whiting studied medicine and practiced as a physician in Hartford. He moved to Great Barrington in 1765, possibly to assume the medical practice of the town's two doctors who had died the previous year.[9] Whiting soon became involved in civic affairs and had been a delegate to the Berkshire County convention in 1774 which drafted a series of proposals opposing the British government. Only a year before Mumbet's trial, Whiting became judge of the court of common pleas for the entire county of Berkshire. No one could be sure how Whiting might impact the proceedings or influence the jury.

All eyes turned to the county courthouse, which stood at the junction of Main and Castle streets in the middle of Great Barrington. The courthouse had been built at a cost of 150 pounds—50 pounds more than the initial budget set aside for its completion.[10] It was, according to town historian Charles Taylor, "destitute of architectural pretention or ornament, save a semi-circular window in its eastern gable and some little carved wood work about the front door."[11] Through a curious quirk in its construction, the building overflowed onto the town's main street.[12] Thus, Mumbet's fate would be determined by a group of Berkshire farmers in a simple, unpainted, wooden edifice of 30 by 40 feet, a mere story and a half tall.

The days become shorter in Berkshire County, as summer begins to wind down. The temperature, which can rise to 90 degrees Fahrenheit in early

August, begins to recede later in the month. As the sun sets earlier each evening, the air becomes cool and crisp. Morning dew settling on the fields of Berkshire in August signals that the autumn harvest lies just around the bend.

We can imagine the team of Sedgwick and Reeve arguing for Brom and Bett before a jury of Berkshire farmers. There, on a late August afternoon, a slight breeze may have blown through the courthouse. Standing before the jury of Jonathan Holcomb and his fellows, Sedgwick, with his beaming black eyes and persuasive voice, held the jury in the palm of his hands. And if we strain to listen very closely, we might hear a few softly spoken—yet profound—points of law uttered by Tapping Reeve.

On what basis did Noble and Canfield defend Ashley? Could it have been on the narrow grounds that Ashley owned the slaves through his wife's inheritance of her father's estate? Or might it have been that Ashley claimed to have purchased Bett and Brom in the nearby slave market of Albany, and that he was therefore entitled, by custom, to own the slaves in perpetuity? Massachusetts common law had long been silent regarding how long slaves could be kept in captivity. White indentured servants, by custom, gained their freedom through a process of working for their owners for a specified period, in most cases from seven to ten years. For African slaves, on the other hand, the length of servitude was often left to their owner's discretion. Though laws were never passed to ensure perpetual servitude of African slaves, owners, by custom, assumed they had such rights. Since there had never been a law passed that allowed slaves to be held in perpetuity, I believe it is likely that Sedgwick and Reeve drove this point home to the jury.

Could Mumbet, in her humble and self-effacing manner, have been called to testify on her own behalf? Could she have relayed to the jury the mistreatment she received at the hands of John Ashley's wife, Hannah Hogeboom? Might the legal team have mentioned Zack Mullen, and sought to clarify the act of trespass he claimed in his own suit filed against John Ashley only several months before?

The teams' arguments to the jury will forever remain a mystery, for the trial log reveals only the facts of the case and, regrettably, neither the line of reasoning advanced by Sedgwick and Reeve, nor the basis on which the judge and jury made their decision.

Years later, a certain Duke de la Rochefoucault Liancourt visited New England and spent time in the home of Theodore Sedgwick. In his book, *Travels Through the United States of North America*, published in London in 1799, he recalls that Sedgwick's argument was two-fold: first, that the laws of Massachusetts never gave slavery legal sanction, and second, that even if they had been interpreted to construe that slavery was permissible, it was obviated by the Constitution of 1780, which held that all men are free and equal. Thus any laws enacted prior to this new document were to be considered null and void. [13]

We know only that Sedgwick and Reeve convinced the jury that Mumbet and Brom could not be considered Ashley's property for life, and that they had been, in fact, illegally detained in bondage. The jury awarded Brom and Bett "the sum of thirty shillings lawful Silver Money Damages And the Costs of this Suit Taxed at five pounds fourteen Shillings and four pence like Money."[14] No doubt, a broad smile formed across the countenance of Mumbet as the jury returned their verdict.

Ashley and his son immediately filed an appeal. Reflecting further on their prospects for success, they decided a short time later to "confess judgment" and abide by the court's decision. Could they have concluded that the Supreme Judicial Court of Massachusetts would reach the same verdict, as slavery was becoming impossible to defend in a court of law? Whatever the reasoning applied to award Bett and Brom their freedom, slave owners throughout the Commonwealth took note, and no doubt many mulled over how or whether they could retain ownership of their slaves.

Four months after Mumbet's trial, a hundred miles to the east of Great Barrington, a slave-for-sale advertisement ran in the pages of the *Boston Gazette* for a "woman in her thirties, capable of all House Hold Business, either in Town or Country."[15] Nearly two-thousand similar ads had been listed in the paper's pages over the last sixty-three years. It would be the last of its kind the newspaper would ever run.

Freedom

Mumbet knew she could not remain in the Ashley home. Though her sister Lizzie remained in the service of the Ashleys, Mumbet had a better offer, as a maid and governess to Theodore Sedgwick, his wife, and their children. Moving across town, she joined the Sedgwick household, where, over time, she became an essential member of the family. Mumbet also became something of a celebrity in Sheffield for having taken on the town's most powerful citizen. Soon after gaining her freedom, she adopted the legal name of Elizabeth Freeman. Living as a free woman in the Sedgwick home, Mumbet became a part of Berskhire County's free black community, which provided a contrast to those who remained enslaved.

When she arrived at the home of Theodore and Pamela Sedgwick, there were already three young children to care for. Elizabeth Mason, born a year after the couple was married, was named after Theodore's first wife. A few years later, the couple added two sons, Frances, and then Theodore, who was born in 1780, a year before Mumbet's freedom suit. In the years before Bett joined the Sedgwick family, Theodore and Pamela had lost three children in childbirth, including a girl who died a day after she was born, and two young infants who lived less than a year.[1] Bett knew that her expertise as a midwife would be needed.

Getting acclimated to her new role was no simple task. As anxious as she was to repay her debt to Theodore Sedgwick for delivering her freedom, she knew her role would hinge on her relationship with Pamela. Bett knew that Pamela was strong-minded and strong-willed. There was some indication that she had married Theodore over the objections of her mother, who was unsure whether his religious background and social stature were on a par with that of her family.[2] All indications are that Bett and Pamela developed a strong relationship. To be sure, Pamela had her hands full and needed all of the help Bett could provide. Most important, Bett knew she would have a stable home for her daughter, who was nicknamed Little Bett.

At about the same time that Bett gained her freedom, Quock Walker, a black slave living in Worcester, some fifty miles to the east of Sheffield, tried to achieve his. Neither Bett nor Walker knew of each other's situation, but they shared a common destiny. The Name Quock, or Quarko, as he was sometimes called, came from the Ghanan phrase meaning *child born on Saturday.* Quock's owner, James Caldwell, had promised him as a child that he would be set free at the age of twenty-five. Some years later, Caldwell died unexpectedly. Walker later moved to the nearby town of Barre, Massachusetts, with Caldwell's widowed wife Isabel, who had since remarried a certain

Nathaniel Jennison. When Isabel died, Quock became the property of Nathaniel Jenison.

While Quock Walker may have thought it was possible that he would one day gain his freedom from the Caldwells, he knew that Nathaniel Jennison would never allow it. Frustrated and angered over the hand he had been dealt, Walker vowed he would not remain in perpetual servitude to Jennison—or to anyone else. With little to lose, Walker ran away from the Jennison homestead, and decided to return to the only family he ever knew.

When Walker arrived at the doorstep of John and Seth Caldwell, the brothers of his deceased owner, he felt the satisfaction of having taken matters into his own hands. Surely the Caldwell brothers would understand his plight. Walker was later abducted by his former owner, beaten, and held in captivity. He was able to escape with the assistance of the Caldwells.

Quock Walker was evidently an extremely productive field hand, for Nathaniel Jennison's suit against the Caldwells called for the outrageous sum of 1,000 pounds lost compensation during Walker's absence.

Walker, who was twenty-seven years old at the time, remained suspended in a state of legal limbo for two years, as attorneys argued over whether he should remain enslaved. Attorney Levi Lincoln gave Walker a glimmer of hope when he shifted his argument away from the alleged facts of the case to something a great deal more powerful, when he stated: "This Quock is our brother. We all had one common origin, descended from the same kind of flesh, had the same breath of life . . . Is it not a law of nature that all men are equal and free? Is not the law of nature the law of G-d? Is not the law of G-d then, against slavery?"[3]

The case was finally brought before William Cushing, the chief justice of the supreme judicial court in Massachusetts. Cushing, the son and grandson of colonial judges in Massachusetts, became an associate judge when his father resigned four years before the start of the American Revolution. The younger Cushing survived his post only after he pledged his allegiance to the Patriot cause. He was elected chief justice of the Massachusetts court in the midst of the Revolutionary War.

Cushing had been a slave owner in the past. However, like Theodore Sedgwick and other converts to the cause of abolition, he freed his slaves. After reflecting on the many arguments advanced in several cases relating to Quock Walker's fate, Cushing ruled resoundingly in his favor:

> Slavery is in my judgment as effectively abolished as it can be by the granting of rights and privileges wholly incompatible and repugnant to its existence. The court are therefore fully of the opinion that perpetual servitude can no longer be tolerated in our government.[4]

Since Cushing was one of five judges ruling on the Quock Walker case, it was unclear whether his instructions to the jury carried the legal weight to end slavery throughout Massachusetts. The silence of the legislature on the matter created confusion in some quarters.

Despite the court's ruling in the Mumbet and Quock Walker trials, slavery continued, albeit in a diminished form, throughout Massachusetts and New England. Slaves in Massachusetts and throughout

New England experienced several outcomes: some were freed and began to be paid for their services. Some slave owners chose a cynical path. In his *History of Wilbraham*, a town in western Massachusetts, a certain Chauncey Edwin Peck recalled that some slaves "were invited to accompany 'massa' on a visit to Hartford, and were privately sold and invited to go on board a sloop lying at the wharf, to have a good time, and while fiddling and dancing, the sloop dropped into the stream, spread sail, and disappeared down the river [and] they were never heard of again."[5]

Mumbet remained dedicated to the Sedgwick family, and continued to offer her services as the family grew. The Sedgwicks gave birth to another son, Henry, in 1785, named after his own brother, who had died in early childhood only six months before.[6]

Theodore Sedgwick began to prosper as an attorney and continued his pursuit of politics. The one-time slave owner and attorney for Elizabeth Freeman continued to undergo a process of awakening, in which he became active in the cause of abolition. In 1785, he joined the Pennsylvania Abolition Society, a group founded by the Quakers, and among the first to protest slavery.

Toward the end of 1785, Theodore Sedgwick purchased land from the Stockbridge Indians, and built a new home that would accommodate his growing family. In the winter of 1785 and 1786, the family, which now included Mumbet, moved to this new home, some ten miles to the north of Sheffield. Yet trouble lay ahead for Mumbet and the Sedgwick family as a new rebellion began to spread through the land. And unlike the American Revolution, when Berkshire County was spared as a battleground, this time she would not be so lucky.

A Family in Need

Less than a year after Mumbet moved from Sheffield to Stockbridge, Berkshire County became engulfed in the crisis that came to be known as Shays' Rebellion. Mumbet would be forced to choose sides in a civil war that divided a fragile state along class lines. Her loyalty to the Sedgwick family would be tested in a most unusual way.

Farmers and artisans returning to their villages in western Massachusetts after the Revolutionary War faced financial ruin amid growing civil unrest. The cost of the war had nearly forced the state into bankruptcy. Creditors pursued their claims—often ruthlessly—against debtors through the young nation's county courts. In central and western Massachusetts, trade suddenly "came to a paralytic halt, labor could find no employment, and entire communities found themselves reduced to the level of barter."[1]

The injustice of the law and the scarcity of hard currency created a cauldron of unrest. Having fought for what they believed was a just cause, former soldiers found themselves unjustly placed in jail. They turned their wrath against the same government whose independence they had fought to achieve.

Daniel Shays, the 39-year-old leader of the rebellion, was a decorated veteran of the Revolutionary War who had fought with distinction at the Battle of Bunker Hill, the second Battle of Saratoga in 1777, and at the Battle of Stony Point, New York in 1779. A year later he resigned his commission and settled in Pelham, Massachusetts. In recognition of his contribution to the Patriot cause Shays was among an elite group of officers selected to receive ceremonial swords from General Lafayette. Shays later incurred the wrath of his fellow Patriots when, for reasons not entirely known, he sold his sword. His decision led his critics to question his allegiance to the American government.

The rebellion began when men gathered in Worcester County in the middle of August, 1786, and drafted a list of eight grievances, calling for, among other things, payment of the public debt.[2] A week later, a convention in Hatfield passed nineteen resolutions in three days. The rebels, or *regulators*, as they were called, railed against the courts and legislature, but "advised the people to abstain from mob violence."[3] They began to target the courts to prevent the injustice they perceived.

On the last Tuesday of August, insurgents bearing swords and muskets converged on the court of common pleas in Northampton, some forty miles east of Stockbridge. The rebels prevented the court from gathering, and forced it to adjourn for the next several months. What began in Worcester and Hampshire counties soon spread west to Berkshire.[4] As summer turned to fall, insurgents shut down the county court in Great Barrington, and forced open the doors of its jail. As prisoners fled their overcrowded quarters, the rebels began house-to-house searches. As a legislator and a frequent litigator before the court, Theodore Sedgwick took the unusual step of safeguarding his papers in the home of a certain Reverend West, his minister.[5]

As autumn receded, and winter stepped in to fill its void, the rebels fought against local militia in West Stockbridge, only a few miles from Mumbet's new home. Sedgwick, according to tradition, led a group of fellow townsmen who forced the rebels to lay down their arms in an open field. Eighty-four prisoners were captured.[6] At about the same time, the Shaysites attacked the federal arsenal in Springfield in an effort to capture badly needed munitions. A late afternoon encounter with federal troops led by Major General Benjamin Lincoln left four of the insurgents lying dead in the snow.

The rebels pursued a list of targets that included the "ruffled shirts"—a label they applied to the lawyers and judges who had sentenced their comrades to prison. Some rebels sought hostages, others looked for firearms and plunder. With its resplendent federal architecture—a symbol of the wealth resented by the Shaysites—the home and person of Theodore Sedgwick became an obvious target.

The Shaysites made more than one attempt to attack Sedgwick at his home. Defending against them called for creative tactics and imagination in order to match their ingenuity. Mumbet provided both. She volunteered to keep the family and neighbors' jewelry locked in an iron chest beside her bed.[7] She favored firing a few pistol shots to alarm the marauders. But, in at least one instance, she was overruled by Pamela Sedgwick.[8]

Respectful of her wishes, Mumbet modified her tactics, and instead greeted visitors at the door—with a lantern in one hand—and a "large kitchen shovel in the other." In another moment of defense, Bett kept the intruders at bay by suspending a boiling kettle of beer above the doorway and threatening to "scald to death the first invader." Mumbet informed the Shaysites that Theodore Sedgwick was nowhere to be found, yet they insisted on searching the house. When they stumbled upon Mumbet's personal chest, one of them asked what was in it. "Oh, you had better search that," Mumbet responded. "An old nigger's chest!" she continued. "You are such gentlemen; you had better search that—the old nigger's as you call me." With these self-effacing words, attributed to her by Electa Jones, the town historian of Stockbridge who described the encounter some 70 years later, Mumbet went on to "shame them" out of stealing the family's silver.[9]

The rebels may have been more interested in Sedgwick's supply of spirits than the jewels. In one instance, they broke open a bottle of porter. Bett threatened retribution with her kitchen shovel. They heeded her warning, in no small part because of their reaction to the wine, which had been marking time in the Sedgwick cellar. One of them said: "if gentlemen liked such cursed, bitter stuff, they might keep it."[10]

Mumbet sympathized with the insurgents, among whose members were the homeless and downtrodden. She knew they were not as dangerous as they made themselves out to be. She took pity on one who returned to the Sedgwick home in search of his boots which had been left behind during a raid. When Pamela Sedgwick, from atop the stairs, asked who was in the house, Mumbet said, "Why, it's nobody but Jim . . . the fellow that came along peddling brooms—miserable things, they are all in the cellar now, I never could use one of them." [11]

The last battle of Shays' Rebellion took place in late February, 1787, when a force of eighty men led by John Ashley's oldest son, also named John, the codefendant in Mumbet's freedom suit, killed or captured a band of rebels in the village of Sheffield.

As the rebellion drew to a close Mumbet turned her attention to helping raise the children of Theodore and Pamela Sedgwick. In 1789, the Sedgwicks gave birth to their third daughter, Catharine Maria. Mumbet recalled that Catharine at her birth was "as fair as a London doll." Of all the Sedgwick children, Catharine would become closest to Mumbet, and would memorialize her in numerous ways. Her presence, Catharine later recalled, was "quite as much rule as service," for Bett "was in truth a sort of nurse-governante in his house—an anomalous office in our land." The Sedgwick children regarded her rule, "as the Jews did theirs, as a theocracy."[12] Eventually, a strong mutual respect developed between this newly anointed monarch and the Sedgwick children.

Catharine recalled Mumbet's motherly counsel during many periods of her childhood, and generally regarded her as a calming influence in her life. As a child, Catharine was shaken by the marriage of her older sister, whom, she realized, would leave the house forever, thus bringing to a close a chapter in their treasured relationship. During the exchange of vows, Catharine cried out in anguish over the fear of losing her sister. It was Mumbet who came to her assistance by delivering a direct, but loving "hush," helping her realize that the situation might not be as devastating as she had feared.[13]

Catharine later recalled:

> In my childhood I clung to her with instinctive love and faith, and the more I know and observe of human nature, the higher does she rise above

> others, whatever may have been their instruction or accomplishment. In her the image of her Maker was cast in material so hard and pure that circumstances could not alter its outline or cloud its luster.[14]

Theodore Sedgwick's political career began to thrive. In the spring of 1787, Sedgwick won election to the Continental Congress, where he would serve for the next twelve years. During that period he spent a great deal of time in New York and Philadelphia, as the federal capital shifted from one city to the next. His dedication to the federal cause kept him away from home almost half the time.[15]

When he was home, Sedgwick remained highly sought after for his legal expertise and compassion for those enslaved. He would later intervene on behalf of one of Bekshire County's legendary characters, Agrippa Hull, a free black, who hailed from the town of Northampton. Hull had found his way to Berkshire County and had enlisted in the Patriot Army. After the war he was employed by Sedgwick. During that period Hull fell in love with Darby, a woman enslaved by one of the area's local residents. Sedgwick intervened and persuaded her owners, a family in Lenox, to free her.[16] Agrippa Hull married Darby in 1795.

In the meantime, Pamela Sedgwick's mental state had begun to deteriorate. The roots of her depression appear to be traceable to the death of her mother, and aggravated by Theodore's absence from home.[17] Pamela suffered several bouts with depression, each of which lasted several months.[18] One of these episodes was so severe that she was sent to the nearby town of Richmond, where she was treated "judiciously and most kindly" by a local physician.[19] Acutely aware of his wife's condition, and the unproven means of improving it, Sedgwick sought relief from many sources, leaving no stone unturned in a quest to alleviate her suffering.[20]

Catharine, keenly aware of the primitive nature of existing treatments of mental illness, recalled that Mumbet was the only one who could "tranquillize my mother when her mind was disordered—the only one of her friends whom she liked to have about her—and why? She treated her with the same respect she did when she was sane. As far as was possible, she obeyed her commands and humored her caprices; in short, her superior instincts hit upon the mode of treatment that science has since adopted."[21]

In the aftermath of her mother's death, Pamela's physical strength had declined mightily, due to having cared for six young children, three of whom were less than five years of age.[22] Pamela Sedgwick was under unusual strain as she prepared to deliver Charles, the couple's tenth and last child, in 1791. Charles' was evidently a difficult birth, and his survival was by no means assured, given the temper of the times, and his fragile condition. For her unusually strong role as a midwife during the birth, Sedgwick gave Mumbet a silver coin, which according to family tradition, she kept until her death.[23]

Ironically, it may have been Theodore Sedgwick who unwittingly contributed to his wife's depression, for his long periods away from home in pursuit of a political career only worsened what may have been her natural tendency toward the disease. Theodore

Sedgwick remained fearful of Pamela falling prey once again to her mental anguish. He provided counsel to his children from afar, when he wrote:

> Read to her, or persuade her to read diverting books. Every other object must submit attention to her. Is company diverting, she must be indulged with it. Does it increase her gloom, it must be kept from her. She is the best of human beings, and every circumstance of business or of pleasure must be made to submit to her restoration.[24]

Sedgwick's letters to his children reveal, among other things, a certain degree of fatalism when he wrote, ". . . I feel that this life is far from affording felicity."[25]

Theodore Sedgwick's career in the U.S. Congress would reach its peak when he was elected Speaker of the House in the autumn of 1799, just before the capital was moved to Washington, D.C. Sedgwick, a great admirer of George Washington, was evidently close to the president, and helped him pass key legislation through the Congress. According to family tradition, Sedgwick was among those who dined with Washington at the end of his second term. During one of Washington's last official dinners, Sedgwick was urged, along with his colleagues, to give assistance to John Adams, the nation's second president, and one of Sedgwick's fellow New England Federalists.

Sensitive to Pamela's deteriorating condition and the needs of his children, Sedgwick decided, instead, to return to Stockbridge. Less than two years later he was appointed justice to the state's Supreme Court. The new position required regular travel to Boston.

Instinctively aware that Theodore Sedgwick's return from the nation's capital would begin a new chapter in the family history, Mumbet began to consider her independence from the family. With savings accumulated through her service to the Sedgwicks, she purchased land and built a home of her own in Stockbridge, only two years after Sedgwick began his term on the bench.

Mumbet's situation stood in stark contrast to many blacks who remained enslaved in Connecticut, Massachusetts' neighbor to the south. One need look no further than Litchfield, Connecticut, some forty miles south of Stockbridge. The *Litchfield Monitor* ran an ad on October 18, 1797, in which a woman of mixed-race origin, who had eight years and six months remaining on her contract of indentured servitude was placed for sale. As "Her present owner not having sufficient employ for her, she will be sold on easy terms at the moderate price of 34 pounds, payable by installments, in sheep or young cattle, for two thirds, the residue in cash." [26]

Though she would remain close to the Sedgwicks and continue to be employed by them, Mumbet began to reclaim her own life and rededicate herself to her growing family. Having repaid her debt to Theodore Sedgwick, by ensuring the safety of his wife and of his children, she was ready to assert her freedom and gradually explore a life of her own.

A Life of Her Own

Throughout her adult life, Mumbet remained highly sought after as a midwife and nurse. Theodore Sedgwick's son later recalled that in this capacity "she had no competitor. I believe she never lost a child, when she had the care of its mother, at its birth. When a child, wailing in the arms of its mother, heard her steps on the stairway, or approaching the door, it ceased to cry."[1]

Mumbet may not have been as fortunate in her own child-bearing. Miscarriages and infant mortality occurred all too frequently in the late eighteenth century. As if to underscore the pain and grief of losing an infant at birth, many family records remain silent on the topic. Mumbet may have lost two children of her own in early childbirth. Records in the Stockbridge cemetery memorialize Bub and "sister to Bub, colored children of MumBett." [2]

This leads us to speculate whether Mumbet married for a second time. W. E. B. Du Bois, the famed intellectual and civil rights leader who hailed from Great Barrington, twice claimed an ancestral link to Mumbet. In *Darkwater*, Dr. Du Bois, Harvard University's first black Ph.D. and a founder of the NAACP, claimed that she was a cousin of his grandmother. In *Dusk of Dawn*, he asserted that Mumbet was the second wife of his great-grandfather, Jacob Burghardt, a free black of Great Barrington. Burghardt, born circa 1760, married his first wife, Violet, "who brought with her an African song which became traditional in the family." [3]

Burghardt and his wife gave birth to nine children, one of whom was Du Bois's grandfather.[4] Du Bois wrote that after Violet died, Jacob married "Mom Bett," who by then had become a celebrity within the town of Stockbridge.[5] That Du Bois would claim a direct connection to Mumbet bears testimony to the esteem in which she was held.

Beginning in 1803, Mumbet purchased five acres of land, very close to the Sedgwick family's home. Importantly, Jonah Humphrey is listed on the land deeds, which are housed in the Berkshire Middle District Registry of Deeds. A second deed indicates that Mumbet's land holdings had grown to nearly nineteen acres. It is likely that she enjoyed "an unhindered view of the northern face of Monument Mountain."[6] A review of the records clearly identifies Elizabeth Freeman as a "single woman," or "spinster," while Jonah Humphrey is referred to as a "laborer." It appears likely that Jonah Humphrey was the husband of Mumbet's daughter. [7]

Mumbet began to enjoy her family, and the company of her daughter, Elizabeth. Mumbet was said to have been an indulgent and loving grandmother who took great pride in her extended family, which included Marianne Dean, her granddaughter, to whom she would one day leave a "purple and white gown—a striped gown, a figured chintz short gown, one pair of coarse cotton stockings, and an umbrella." Her last will reveals great-granddaughters Anne Dean, Mary Elizabeth Dean, Lydia Maria, and a great-grandson, Amos Josiah, to whom she left a "large red chest writing desk the bedstead and bedding he now uses, two colored bordered handkerchiefs and one dessert spoon." [8]

Bett continued to enjoy her freedom, family and property, living in Stockbridge, which in her later years, included a thriving free black community, probably the largest of its kind in Western Massachusetts. No matter how trying her circumstances later in life, Mumbet never forgot her humble origins, nor would she have ever agreed to return to her former master. She was known to have expressed the sentiment: "Any time, any time while I was a slave, if one minute's freedom had been offered to me, and I had been told I must die at the end of that minute, I would have taken it—just to stand one minute on god' *airth* a free woman—I would." [9]

Yet, Mumbet refused to break her ties to the Sedgwick family. She continued to watch over Pamela Sedgwick as her health continued along a steady decline and she began to fall prey to the sickness that had long afflicted her. In September of 1807, one of the Sedgwick's neighbors, a certain Mary Bidwell, noted in a letter that Mumbet "was alarmed while dressing [Pamela] that morning by the appearance of a livid spot over her right eye." [10] Another neighbor noted that Pamela Sedgwick retired to bed that evening "without special complaint." [11] That same night, against the silhouette of a full moon that lit the early autumn sky, Pamela Sedgwick succumbed to her affliction.[12] It was a long night for a woman who had experienced so much suffering in her life, as she felt the pain of "twenty distressing paroxysms" that brought about her end.[13] Messengers traveled west to Albany and east to Boston to alert members of the Sedgwick family of Pamela's passing.

Mumbet sought to comfort Catharine, who, in her eighteenth year, was inconsolable at her mother's death. When all else failed, Mumbet tried to shake

Catharine into looking at her mother's life in a wider context. "We must be quiet," she advised. "Don't you think I am grieved? Our hair has grown white together." [14]

A week before Theodore Sedgwick married for the third time, in 1808, Mumbet informed the family that she would be leaving their service.[15] Out of loyalty to Pamela Sedgwick, the woman for whom she had cared for many years, and who had been deceased for a little less than a year, and sensing that she would be required to pay homage to Sedgwick's new wife, Bett knew it would be better to bow out of the family's affairs.

A few years later, Mumbet was stricken by the loss of her beloved granddaughter, who "died without an instant's warning." At the time of her death, Catharine Sedgwick recalled that Mumbet's entire family was deeply afflicted, and though Mumbet was "the most calm among them," she was also "the most deeply wounded." [16] But Mumbet could not contain her emotions for long when faced with the stark reality of her deceased granddaughter. As she held her shroud after the funeral, Mumbet "burst into an overwhelming torrent of expressions." Deeply distraught over the loss of the little girl for whom she had so much hope, she cried out: "I dressed you first, and I dressed you last."[17] Catharine Sedgwick later recalled that Mumbet paced up and down the room "with her hands knit together and great tears rolling down her cheeks, repeating as if to send back into her soul its swelling sorrow, 'Don't say a word,' it's G-d's will!"[18]

Though Mumbet elected to live out her days in her home in Stockbridge, she was never far from Catharine and her siblings. Nor was she forgotten by them. Frances Sedgwick Watson, writing to her brothers Henry and Robert, nine years after the death of their natural mother, informed them that "Our faithful and good old Mother is the nurse of comfort of Charles' sick lad—she sends her love to you and Harry."[19]

Mumbet would live to see Catharine Sedgwick publish her first three novels, *A New England Tale* (1822), *Redwood: A Tale* (1824), and *Hope Leslie*

(1827). Catharine would eventually write more than fifteen books and over 100 short stories. Mumbet would certainly have taken satisfaction in knowing that she had exercised a maternal influence over one of America's most prolific and influential writers.

Even though Mumbet did not live with them, the Sedgwick family watched over her, and insisted that she be cared for by the leading physicians of Stockbridge. Dr. Albert Hopkins was one who watched over Mumbet in her later years. In September, 1829, only two months before her death, Albert wrote that he, along with his brother Harry and two other doctors, had visited Mumbet to see how they might be of assistance. The doctors had evidently gathered for an informal conclave, in which they compared notes on a variety of plants, roots, and other medicinal remedies common to the period. Albert Hopkins noted that the doctors had spent the evening with Mumbet "until nearly eleven at night . . . ," adding with emphasis, "*it beat all I can tell you.*" [20]

Less than two weeks later, Mark Hopkins, a third Hopkins brother, who later became president of

Williams College, wrote his brother Harry that he had been informed that the doctors had alleviated Mumbet's ailment, which was evidently traceable to a type of swelling.[21] Mark Hopkins wrote, "I would give a copper to know" what the doctors did to improve Mumbet's condition.[22] Harry informed him a month later that "Mumbet is alive but failing, the ulcer is entirely healed."[23] He went on to note that one of the doctors had used "the Baptista tinctoriam applied to the Ulcer as I understood and taken internally."[24]

In October of 1829, Mumbet compiled her last will and testament with the help of Catharine's brother Charles, who at the time was living in Lenox. In it, Mumbet left half of her land holdings to her daughter Elizabeth and her heirs, and the other half to two of her great-grandchildren, Amos Josiah Van Schaach, and Lydia Maria Ann Van Schaach, and their heirs. Mumbet left the rest of her worldly possessions to them and to three other great-granddaughters.

Exactly one month later, Catharine Sedgwick

made an entry to her diary that demonstrated just how distraught she was over Mumbet's declining condition: "Mumbet—Mother—my nurse—my faithful friend—she who first received me into her arms—is finishing her career . . . she could not forgive a wrong, but she would sooner have died at the stake than committed it."[25] In a letter dated November 18, Mark Hopkins wrote to his brother Harry, giving his candid, if pessimistic assessment: "I hear that Mumbet is not like to recover, notwithstanding the conclave—.[26]

Charles wrote to Catharine in mid-December, 1829, noting that he had recently visited with Mumbet, having "been prevented from going by a violent storm yesterday."[27] He reported, "When I saw Mumbet she was calm and perfectly self-possessed tho she has I understand at times been somewhat delirious—she inquired 'how they all did in New York' and twice particularly after you." Charles went on to write that "she is confined to her bed suffers a good deal of pain & is very desirous to get at the end of her trials & when I said to her that it was a comfort to think that the time which now seemed so long seems very short to look back upon she said 'O yes it was a great comfort.' "[28]

Toward the end of her days, David Dudley Field, who served as the minister for Stockbridge's Congregational church, visited Mumbet. He asked, "Are you afraid to meet your G-d?" Mumbet replied, No, Sir. I am not afeard. I have tried to do my duty, and I am *not* afeard!" [29]

Mumbet passed away on Tuesday morning December 28th at 8:00 AM. Charles Sedgwick provides a vivid description of her funeral, which he shared with his sister Catharine in a letter written on New Year's day. "I wish dear sister," he wrote, "that you could have stood by me, and enjoyed with me, in looking upon her great and noble face, tranquil and beautiful as it seemed to me." [30]

He continued, "There was one thing about her face which I believe is uncommon in a person of her age and it was very striking—Her brow and forehead were as smooth as an infant's it seemed to me a fit emblem of the repose which should come at the close of such a life & a beautiful message of her joyful tranquility with which such a spirit should return to G-d who gave it . . ."

The Sedgwick family chose to bury her in the family plot in Stockbridge, no doubt an act of devotion, and a reminder to future generations of the role she played in keeping the family together. The family plot, which has since come to be called the Sedgwick Pie, is unique in that Theodore and Pamela Sedgwick are interred in the middle of what has become a well thought-out series of concentric rings. The arrangement was, according to novelist and family member John Sedgwick, "based on the Romantic ideal of the circle," with the "children's graves resting at their parents' feet and facing inward, reverentially, toward them." [31]

Fourteen months after Mumbet passed away, Theodore Sedgwick, Catharine's brother, accepted an invitation to speak before a group gathered at the Berkshire Athaneum. In an address entitled "Practicability of the Abolition of Slavery," Sedgwick, referring to Mumbet, stated "If there could be a practical refutation of the imagined natural superiority of our race to hers, the life and character of this woman would afford that refutation . . . she had nothing of the submissive or the subdued character, which succumbs to superior force, and is the usual result of the state of slavery. On the contrary, without ever claiming superiority, she, uniformly, in every case, obtained an ascendancy over all those with whom she was associated in service." [32]

In response to those in the community or elsewhere who had their doubts about African people, Sedgwick boldly asserted in the same address: "Having known this woman as familiarly as I knew either of my parents, I cannot believe in the moral or physical inferiority of the race to which she belonged." [33]

The winter months in New England last longer than most would prefer, though one can argue that they are among its most beautiful. The reflection of the sun over freshly fallen snow lying below a clear blue sky reminds one of the reasons for living here.

The village of Stockbridge, with its tree-lined streets and historic homes, remains faithful in disposition to its timeless roots. A stroll from the Red Lion Inn along Main Street leads to the cemetery where Mumbet rests through the ages. Graying gravestones set side by side sit silently as the seasons change. Walking through a winding path, ascending along a steady incline, we come upon Mumbet's grave site, situated inside the innermost circle of the Sedgwick Pie. Standing before the stone we read what became of Catharine Sedgwick's note, composed almost two hundred years ago:

> ELIZABETH FREEMAN. Known by the name of Mumbet. Died December 28, 1829. Her supposed age was eighty-five years. She could neither read nor write, yet in her own sphere, she had no superior or equal. She neither wasted time nor property. She never violated a trust, nor failed to perform a duty. In every situation of domestic trial she was the most efficient helper and the tenderest friend. Good mother, farewell.

Epilogue

Mumbet's legacy lives on in many forms. Those interested in walking in her footsteps can visit the Colonel John Ashley House in Sheffield, Massachusetts, where she spent a portion of her life enslaved in his home. The house is maintained by the Trustees of Reservations, an organization known for its preservation of open land and landmark properties. The Ashley House is also part of the Upper Housatonic Valley African American Heritage Trail, which features forty-eight sites in twenty-nine towns, including the W.E.B. Du Bois childhood home, a national landmark property in Great Barrington.

One can still observe the Sedgwick home in Sheffield. It is likely the place where Mumbet first approached Sedgwick with the idea to pursue her freedom. The house is located on Main Street, in downtown Sheffield, and is distinguished by its stately Greek columns. The site of Mumbet's trial at the corner of Main Street and Castle Street is now the Great Barrington Town Hall. Each year in August, the Sheffield Historical Society sponsors the annual "Mumbet Walk to Freedom,"a four mile trek from the Ashley House to the Sedgwick home.

Mumbet's heroic action is memorialized with a statue in the Smithsonian National Museum of African American History and Culture in Washington, D.C. The inscription on her cast figure reads: "Freeman stood up for herself unapologetically. She boldly called attention to the fact that her slave owner, Annetje Ashley, maimed her arm with a hot kitchen shovel." The statue resides in the Slavery and Freedom gallery.

The greatest tribute to Mumbet is the Elizabeth Freeman Center. Founded in 1974, and based in

Pittsfield, Massachusetts, the Center offers hope, help, and healing to anyone affected by domestic or sexual violence. Each year, the Center helps thousands of people across the county with counseling, shelter, safety planning, and legal advocacy.

Theodore Sedgwick pursued a successful career in politics and the law, as a member of the Confederation Congress of 1785-1788. During this period, while at home, he led efforts in deed and in writing, to suppress the Shays Rebellion. An ardent Federalist, he worked to ratify the Constitution during the Massachusetts Convention of 1788. Sedgwick was elected to the first U.S. Congress in 1789, and served three terms. When Alexander Hamilton resigned as Secretary of the Treasury in 1795, Sedgwick was almost tapped as his successor. Sedgwick served briefly in the U.S. Senate, and then became Speaker of the House during the Sixth Congress. He retired from Congress in 1801, and the following year he was appointed to the Supreme Judicial Court of Massachusetts.

Sedgwick maintained an active, life-long correspondence with key Federalist party leaders. He received the last letter ever written by Alexander Hamilton, which he sent on July 10, 1804, only hours before his duel with Aaron Burr on the fields of Weehawken, New Jersey. In the letter, Hamilton expresses his concern over the growing separatist movement in the Federalist party, which contributed to its demise. Sedgwick continued as a judge on the Supreme Judicial Court until his death in 1813.

In 1822, Catharine Maria Sedgwick anonymously published her first novel, *The New England Tale*. Five years later, she wrote her fourth book, *Hope Leslie; or Early Times in The Massachusetts*, a work of historical fiction, whose sympathy for feminism and fairness toward native Americans were well ahead of her time. Eight years later, she authored *The Linwoods, or "Sixty Years Since" in America*, which along with her previous works established her as the premier female author in America. A remarkably prolific writer, she authored sixteen books, and more than 100 short stories. Nathaniel Hawthorne called her "our most truthful novelist." Edgar Allan Poe said that she was "not only one of our most celebrated and most meritorious writers, but attained reputation at a period when American reputation in letters was regarded as a phenomenon."[1] In 1857 she wrote *Married or Single?*, her final novel, in which she rejects society's stigmas assigned to unmarried women. She is buried alongside Mumbet in the Sedgwick Family Pie. Today, the Catharine Maria Sedgwick Society continues to honor and celebrate her life and writing.

Tapping Reeve, Theodore Sedgwick's co-counsel on the *Brom and Bett Vs. Ashley* suit, went on to establish the Litchfield Law School in 1784, only three years after Mumbet gained her freedom. A single-room structure built alongside his home, Reeve's school was the first dedicated to the instruction of American law. It attracted a nationwide student body, with an estimated twenty percent of students coming from the South. His first law student was Aaron Burr, whom he tutored as a child. John C. Calhoun, Noah Webster, and Horace Mann were among

Reeve's most famous students. The school's more than 1,110 attendees included sixteen U.S. senators, fifty congressman, forty justices of state courts, two U.S. Supreme Court Justices, five cabinet members, and ten governors.

Volume I of the lecture notes of one Lonson Nash, a student of Reeve's at the law school, reveals Reeve's personal thoughts on slavery, captured during one of his "Servant and Master" lectures: "Until there is a Charter given from Heaven to our Sea Captains, I shall doubt their right to separate father & mother, brother & sister, bear them into foreign climes, there to linger out a miserable existence in servitude & despair."[2]

A deeply religious man, Reeve was responsible for bringing the Reverend Lyman Beecher (father of Harriet Beecher Stowe) to Litchfield, where he preached for seventeen years. Reeve became Chief Justice of the Connecticut Supreme Court in 1814, only two years before publishing his epic discourse: *The Law of Baron and Femme; Of Parent and Child; of Guardian and Ward; Of Master and Servant; And of the Powers of Courts of Chancery. With an Essay on the Terms; Heir, Heirs, and Heirs of the Body*—book titles of the eighteenth century being considerably less catchy than today. One of the first treatises on family law in the United States, Reeve made the case that women should be permitted to make wills, a point of law widely rejected at the time.

Afterword

I'd like to let the reader know what Mumbet's story means to me personally, and why I decided to write this book. I first became aware of Mumbet while reading Gary Nash's *The Forgotten Fifth: African Americans in the Age of Revolution*. I was struck by Nash's vivid description of a woman who was "all humbleness on the surface but iron underneath." As an eager student of early American history and a frequent traveler to the Berkshires in Western Massachusetts, I was surprised I'd never heard of her. As a child, I had spent several memorable summers at Eisner Camp in Great Barrington, and when I learned that Mumbet's trial had taken place in the town, I began to feel a personal connection to her story.

As I dug deeper into Mumbet's life and times, I discovered an inspiring, courageous woman, who, like Harriet Tubman and Rosa Parks, had taken matters into her own hands, pursuing an ideal, and helping many others along the way. Mumbet's self-effacing manner belied an uncanny intelligence, and an acute awareness of injustice. I was also impressed by her insight into those whose lives she touched. I decided that hers was a story well worth telling.

When I was growing up in the suburbs of New York City, it was gratifying to know that the region played a crucial role in ending slavery. I do not, however, recall any reference to slavery in the Northern states during my high school and college studies. As I began my research on Mumbet, I discovered what was, for me, an unknown chapter in our history. I was deeply disturbed by what I encountered.

The forgotten story of slavery in the New England and Mid-Atlantic colonies has been well-documented thanks to the diligent probing of several scholars, including Dr. Lorenzo Johnston Greene, whose *Negro in Colonial New England: 1620-1776* was first published in 1942. Dr. Greene's book required me to come to terms with having lived in a region that contributed to the rise of slavery, and played an even greater role in sustaining the slave trade.

In the last twenty years or so, the story of slavery and the slave trade in the North has gradually come into focus after decades of neglect. Numerous books have shed light on the subject, including *Complicity: How the North Promoted, Prolonged, and Profited from Slavery,* by Anne Farrow, Joel Lang, and Jenifer Frank; *Sons of Providence*, by Charles Rappleye, *Disowning Slavery* by Joanne Pope Melish, and more recently, *Ten Hills Farm*, by C.S. Manegold, and *Ebony and Ivy*, by Craig Steven Wilder.

The subtitle of this book, *Mumbet and the Roots of Abolition,* is meant to underscore the fact that Mumbet's freedom suit occurred almost two generations before the outset of the Abolitionist movement. Mumbet, along with Theodore Sedgwick, and

Tapping Reeve, the talented attorneys who helped win her freedom, were by no means crusaders in what would become a war to end slavery. Nonetheless, they foresaw the need for racial justice when such views were not in the mainstream, well ahead of their time.

While it was disturbing to learn that slavery existed in the North for well over one hundred years before the American Revolution, it was reassuring to learn that Mumbet's freedom suit occurred fifty years before William Lloyd Garrison published the first issue of *The Liberator*, sixty-four years before Frederick Douglass published his first autobiography, sixty-eight years before Harriet Tubman crossed the line into freedom, and seventy years before Harriet Beecher Stowe's *Uncle Tom's Cabin* appeared in print.

That a jury of farmers living in and around the towns of Great Barrington in Western Massachusetts played a decisive role in determining Mumbet's fate confirmed my faith in the idea that most people will, when given the chance, choose to do the right thing. For me, Mumbet's story is a powerful reminder of the sheer grit required to radically alter, and in this case, topple, an established way of life. It is also a robust reminder that before slavery could be abolished in the South, it needed to be uprooted in the North.

Acknowledgments

I wish to thank Jim Miller of the Sheffield Historical Society, whose book *Early Life in Sheffield Berkshire County, Massachusetts*, provided much insight into the community from which Mumbet emerged. Jim patiently pointed me to many valuable one-of-a-kind documents housed within the Society's collection. Thanks to Barbara Allen of the Stockbridge Public Library for helping me to find materials related to Mumbet and the history of Stockbridge. I benefited much from the writing and research of Bernard Drew, Berkshire County's preeminent historian, whose own *If They Close the Door on You, Go in the Window*, provided critical insights into the region's African-American community. His comprehensive bibliography helped me reconstruct the chronology and events of her life. John Sedgwick's memoir, *In My Blood*, shed much light on Mumbet's impact on the Sedgwick family. As did Timothy Kenslea's *Sedgwicks in Love*. Will Garrison and Barbara Dowling of the Trustees of Reservations graciously commented on the manuscript.

Closer to home, Elizabeth Bouvier of the Massachusetts Judicial Court Archives allowed me to review the original trial log of *Brom & Bett vs. J. Ashley*. I appreciate the assistance of Peter Drummey, librarian of the Massachusetts Historical Society, who helped me locate letters cited in Timothy Kenslea's book, which were housed within the Society's vast collection of Sedgwick family papers. Thanks to Leslie Perrin Wilson of the Concord Public Library, and to Jean Williams of the Lexington Public Library who helped track down many articles relating to slavery in early New England.

Thanks to my parents, Herb and Esther Rose, and to my brother Judah and sister Eve, who encouraged me to pursue my passion for early American history, and to Lisa Cardinal, who provided extraordinary encouragement, and believed—more than anyone else—that Mumbet was worthy of a book of her own.

I wish to express special thanks to Sid Hall, founder of Hobblebush Books, whose editorial acumen and patience were brought to bear on this manuscript many times. In addition, I was fortunate to draw on Sid's expertise in book design. Thanks also to Kirsty Walker, president of Hobblebush Books, for her help throughout this second edition, including the new book cover design.

Finally, I take responsibility for any errors of judgment or of fact which may appear in this book.

Notes & Bibliography

Notes

Chapter 1 · Pain and Promise

1 Catharine M. Sedgwick, "Slavery in New England," 2.

2 Martineau, *Retrospect of Western Travel,* 6.

Chapter 2 · Northern Bondage

1 Greene, *Negro in Colonial New England,* 111.

2 Greene, *Negro in Colonial New England,* 17.

3 Greene, *Negro in Colonial New England,* 21–2.

4 Greene, *Negro in Colonial New England,* 63–5.

5 Higginbotham, *In the Matter of Color,* 62.

6 Moore, *Slavery in Massachusetts,* 73.

7 Farrow, Lang, and Frank, *Complicity,* 62.

8 Greene, *Negro in Colonial New England,* 75.

9 Melish, *Disowning Slavery,* 17.

10 White, *The History of Litchfield,* 153.
11 King, Jr., "I have a Dream Speech"
12 Greene, *Negro in Colonial New England,* 72.
13 Greene, *Negro in Colonial New England,* 171.
14 Deroschers, "Slave for Sale Ads," 623–4.
15 Greene, *Negro in Colonial New England,* 176.
16 Moore, *Slavery in Massachusetts*, 70.
17 Deroschers, "Slave for Sale Ads," 634.
18 Moore, *Slavery in Massachusetts,* 50.
19 Greene and Harrington, *American Population,* 16.
20 Greene, *Negro in Colonial New England,* 72.
21 In Greene and Harrington, *American Population,* the authors note that militia muster roles were multiplied by five to determine the size of the population. The average family size could be estimated at 5.5–6 persons per household in the 1770s, xxii.
22 Writing in 1866, the year after the end of America's Civil War, historian Moore observed: "Some recalled the numbering of Israel by David, and perhaps all were jealous of the possible designs of the Government in England in obtaining accurate information of their numbers and resources. It is a curious fact that the first census in Massachusetts was a census of negro slaves." Moore, *Slavery in Massachusetts,* 50.
23 Piersen, *Black Yankees,* 5.
24 Greene, *Negro in Colonial New England,* 21–2.
25 Greene, *Negro in Colonial New England,* 59.
26 McManus, *Black Bondage in the North,* 10.
27 Greene, *Negro in Colonial New England,* 69.
28 Greene, *Negro in Colonial New England,* 174.
29 Higginbotham, *In the Matter of Color,* 62.

30 Williams, *History of the Negro Race in America,* 228.
31 Higginbotham, *In the Matter of Color,* 84.
32 Hine, *Black Women in America,* 1070–1071.
33 Williams, *History of the Negro Race in America,* 228.
34 Williams, *History of the Negro Race in America,* 228.

Chapter 3 · Berkshire Lives

1 Holland, *History of Western Massachusetts,* Vol. 1, 164.
2 Miller, *Early Life in Sheffield,* 11–12.
3 Miller, *Early Life in Sheffield,* 37.
4 Chase and Chapman, *The Ashleys,* 3.
5 Holland, *History of Western Massachusetts,* Vol. I, 198.
6 Carvalho, *Black Families in Hampden County*, 1.
7 Holland, *History of Western Massachusetts,* Vol. I, 199.
8 Carvalho, *Black Families in Hampden County,* 2.
9 Carvalho, *Black Families in Hampden County,* 2.
10 Wilds, *Mumbet,* 21.
11 Chase and Chapman, *The Ashleys,* 5.
12 Nash, *Forgotten Fifth,* 20.
13 Graham, "The Life and Times of Elizabeth Freeman," 5.
14 Jones, *Stockbridge, Past and Present,* 239.
15 Drew, *If They Close the Door,* 31.
16 Chase and Chapman, *The Ashleys,* 5.
17 Davis, *Inhuman Bondage,* 128–129.
18 Davis, *Inhuman Bondage,* 128.
19 Greene, *Negro in Colonial New England,* 142.
20 Collier, *A History of Old Kinderhook,* 145.
21 Catharine Maria Sedgwick, "Slavery in New England," 2.
22 Catharine Maria Sedgwick, "Slavery in New England," 2.

23 Catharine Maria Sedgwick, "Slavery in New England," 2.
24 Taylor, *Western Massachusetts in the Revolution,* 57–58.
25 Taylor, *History of Great Barrington,* 227.
26 Taylor, *History of Great Barrington,* 227.
27 Welch, *Theodore Sedgwick,* 8.
28 Welch, *Theodore Sedgwick,* 8.
29 "Robert Sedgwick," *Dictionary of American Biography,* 549.
30 "Robert Sedgwick," *Dictionary of American Biography,* 549.
31 Kenslea, *Sedgwicks in Love*, 4.
32 Welch, *Theodore Sedgwick,* 9.
33 Welch, *Theodore Sedgwick,* 9.
34 Welch, *Theodore Sedgwick,* 10.
35 Welch, *Theodore Sedgwick,* 11.
36 Welch, *Theodore Sedgwick,* 11.
37 *The Massachusetts Spy,* February 18, 1773.
38 Holland, *History of Western Massachusetts,* Volume II, 583.
39 Drew, *If They Close the Door,* 31.

Chapter 4 · Awakening

1 Williams, *History of the Negro Race in America,* 220.
2 Williams, History of the Negro Race in America, 221.
3 Rosenthal, "Puritan Conscience and New England Slavery," 72.
4 Rosenthal, "Puritan Conscience and New England Slavery," 73.
5 Rosenthal, "Puritan Conscience and New England Slavery," 75.
6 Kaplan, *Black Presence*, 11.
7 Kaplan, *Black Presence*, 13.

8 Miller, *Early Life in Sheffield,* 74.
9 Moore, *Slavery in Massachusetts,* 186.
10 Moore, *Slavery in Massachusetts,* 191.
11 Moore, *Slavery in Massachusetts,* 193.
12 Moore, *Slavery in Massachusetts,* 194.
13 Moore, *Slavery in Massachusetts,* 194.
14 Higginbotham, *In the Matter of Color,* 89.
15 Higginbotham, *In the Matter of Color,* 90.
16 There has been much debate over whether Mumbet was shielding her sister or her daughter from Hannah Ashley during the infamous kitchen shovel attack. My source for citing the intended victim as Mumbet's sister is Catharine Maria Sedgwick's essay "Slavery in New England," published in Bentley's Miscellany in 1853, in which "Lizzie" is clearly identified as Mumbet's sister. The second source is "Practicality of the Abolition of Slavery," a published lecture delivered by Theodore Sedgwick's son in 1831, in which he also identifies the victim as Mumbet's sister. More detail on these sources may be found in the bibliography.
17 Welch, *Theodore Sedgwick,* 16.
18 Drew, *If They Close the Door,* 30.
19 Drew, *If They Close the Door,* 30.
20 Catharine Maria Sedgwick, "Slavery in New England," 2.
21 Moore, *Slavery in Massachusetts,* 209.
22 Levinson, *African American Heritage,* 17.
23 Catharine Maria Sedgwick, "Slavery in New England," 4.

Chapter 5 · Trial

1 Swanson, "Tapping Reeve," 8.
2 Cross, *The Autobiography of Lyman Beecher*, 162.

3 Cross, *The Autobiography of Lyman Beecher*, 162.
4 Malone, ed., Tapping Reeve portrait in *Dictionary of American Biography*, Vol. 8, 469.
5 Zilversmith, "Mumbet: Folklore and Fact," 11.
6 Zilversmith, "Mumbet: Folklore and Fact," 11
7 Brom and Bett Vs. Ashley, court transcript.
8 Rosenthal, "Free Soil," 784.
9 Taylor, *History of Great Barrington*, 274.
10 Taylor, *History of Great Barrington*, 287.
11 Taylor, *History of Great Barrington*, 288.
12 Taylor, *History of Great Barrington*, 288.
13 Swan, "The Slave Who Sued for Freedom;" Moore, *Notes on Slavery in Massachusetts*, 210–211.
14 Rosenthal, "Free Soil," 785.
15 Deroschers, "Slave for Sale Ads," 664.

Chapter 6 · Freedom

1 Kenslea, *Sedgwicks in Love, 15.*
2 Kenslea, *Sedgwicks in Love, 15.*
3 MacEacheren, "Emancipation in Massachusetts," 290; *Nash, The Forgotten Fifth, 22.*
4 MacEacheren, "Emancipation in Massachusetts," 303.
5 Carvalho, *Black Families in Hampden County*, 4.
6 Kenslea, *Sedgwicks in Love,* 17.

Chapter 7 · A Family in Need

1 Martyn, *Artemas Ward*, 275.
2 Egleston, *Life of General Paterson*, 167.
3 Egleston, *Life of General Paterson*, 167.

4 Egleston, *Life of General Paterson,* 168.
5 Jones, *Stockbridge, Past and Present,* 188.
6 Jones, *Stockbridge, Past and Present,* 190.
7 Martineau, *Retrospect of Western Travel,* 247.
8 Martineau, *Retrospect of Western Travel,* 247.
9 Jones, *Stockbridge, Past and Present,* 194.
10 Martineau, *Retrospect of Western Travel,* 248.
11 Jones, *Stockbridge, Past and Present,* 194.
12 Catharine Maria Sedgwick, "Slavery in New England," 3
13 Kelley, *The Power of Her Sympathy,* 84.
14 Kelley, *The Power of Her Sympathy,* 70.
15 Kenslea, *The Sedgwicks in Love,* 19.
16 Jones, *Stockbridge, Past and Present,* 241.
17 Kenslea, *The Sedgwicks in Love,* 20.
18 Dewey, *Life and Letters of Catharine M. Sedgwick,* 28.
19 Dewey, *Life and Letters of Catharine M. Sedgwick,* 28.
20 Sedgwick, *In My Blood,* 121–2.
21 Dewey, *Life and Letters of Catharine M. Sedgwick,* 29.
22 Kenslea, *The Sedgwicks in Love,* 21.
23 Sedgwick, *In My Blood,* 104–5, 110.
24 Dewey, *Life and Letters of Catharine M. Sedgwick,* 33.
25 Dewey, *Life and Letters of Catharine M. Sedgwick,* 30.
26 White, *The History of Litchfield,* 155.

Chapter 8 · A Life of Her Own

1 Sedgwick, *Abolition of Slavery,* 18.
2 Drew, *If They Close the Door,* 32.
3 Asante, *African Intellectual Heritage,* 415.
4 Asante, *African Intellectual Heritage,* 415.

5 Asante, *African Intellectual Heritage,* 415.

6 Drew, *If They Close the Door,* 33.

7 Enoch Humphrey to Elizabeth Freeman, May 26, 1809, Book 47, Berkshire Middle District Registry of Deeds, 233. In Emilie Piper and David Levinson's *One Minute a Free Woman: Elizabeth Freeman and the Struggle for Freedom*, published in 2010, a year after Mother of Freedom, the authors provide deep insight into black community life in Sheffield and its surrounding towns. The authors have also done much genealogical research on Mumbet's offspring, and succeeding generations of the family. They believe that Jonah Humphrey was, in all likelihood, the husband of Mumbet's daughter.

8 Freeman, "Last Will and Testament."

9 Catharine M. Sedgwick, "Slavery in New England."

10 Kenslea, *The Sedgwicks in Love,* 30.

11 Kenslea, *The Sedgwicks in Love,* 30.

12 Kenslea, *The Sedgwicks in Love,* 30.

13 Kenslea, *The Sedgwicks in Love,* 30.

14 Dewey, *Life and Letters of Catharine M. Sedgwick,* 43.

15 Kenslea, *The Sedgwicks in Love,* 55.

16 Catharine M. Sedgwick to Frances Sedgwick Watson, undated letter in February, 1815, Sedgwick Family Papers, MHS.

17 Catharine M. Sedgwick to Frances Sedgwick Watson, undated letter in February, 1815, Sedgwick Family Papers, MHS.

18 Dewey, *Life and Letters of Catharine M. Sedgwick,* 43.

19 Frances Sedgwick Watson to Henry D. Sedgwick and Robert Sedgwick, Feb. 19, 1817, MHS.

20 Drew, *If They Close the Door,* 33.

21 Drew, *If They Close the Door,* 33
22 Hopkins, *Early Letters of Mark Hopkins,* 197.
23 Hopkins, *Early Letters of Mark Hopkins,* 205.
24 Hopkins, *Early Letters of Mark Hopkins,* 205.
25 Kelley, *The Power of Her Sympathy,* 125.
26 Drew, *If They Close the Door,* 33.
27 Charles Sedgwick to Catharine M. Sedgwick, Dec. 17, 1829, CMS I Papers, MHS.
28 Charles Sedgwick to Catharine M. Sedgwick, Dec. 17, 1829, CMS I Papers, MHS.
29 Kelley, *The Power of Her Sympathy,* 71.
30 Charles Sedgwick to Catharine M. Sedgwick, Jan. 1, 1830, Sedgwick Family Papers, MHS.
31 John Sedgwick, *In My Blood,* 158–9.
32 Sedgwick, *Abolition of Slavery,* 16.
33 Sedgwick, *Abolition of Slavery,* 18–19.

Epilogue

1 Cassidy, "A Prolific Writer Ahead of Her Time."
2 Ireland, "The Rote Notes of Early U.S. Law."

Bibliography

UNPUBLISHED PRIMARY SOURCES

Court Records, letters, and public deeds

Brom and Bett vs. J. Ashley, Esq., August 21, 1781 (Massachusetts State Archives, Boston, MA).

Freeman, Elizabeth. Last Will and Testament, October 18, 1829, typed version in Sheffield Historical Society.

Humphrey, Enoch, to Elizabeth Freeman, May 26, 1809, Berkshire Middle District Registry of Deeds, Book 47, page 233.

Catharine M. Sedgwick to Frances Sedgwick Watson, letter dated in February, 1815, Sedgwick Family Papers, Massachusetts Historical Society.

Robert Sedgwick to Catharine M. Sedgwick, March 28, 1816, Sedgwick Family Papers, Massachusetts Historical Society.

Charles Sedgwick to Catharine M. Sedgwick, Jan. 1, 1830, Sedgwick Family Papers, Massachusetts Historical Society.

Frances Sedgwick Watson to Henry D. Sedgwick and Robert Sedgwick, Feb. 19, 1817, Sedgwick Family Papers, Massachusetts Historical Society.

Catharine M. Sedgwick to Charles Sedgwick, Dec. 17, 1829, Catherine Sedgwick Papers, Massachusetts Historical Society.

BOOKS

Asante, Molefi Kete. *African Intellectual Heritage.* Philadelphia: Temple University Press, 1996.

Carvalho III, Joseph. *Black Families in Hampden County, Massachusetts: 1650–1855.* Westfield, MA: New England Historic Genealogical Society and Institute for Massachusetts Studies, 1984.

Chase, Arthur C. and Gerard Chapman. *The Ashleys, a Pioneer Berkshire Family.* Beverly, MA: The Trustees of Reservations, (circa 1975).

Collier, Edward A. *A History of Old Kinderhook.* New York: G.P. Putnam's Sons, 1914.

Cross, Barbara M., ed. *The Autobiography of Lyman Beecher, Volume I,* Cambridge, MA: The Belknap Press of Harvard University, 1961.

Davis, David Brian. *Inhuman Bondage: The Rise and Fall of Slavery in the New World.* New York: Oxford University Press, 2006.

Dewey, Chester, Rev. *A History of the County of Berkshire, Massachusetts; In Two Parts. The First Being a General View of the County; the Second, An Account of the Several Towns.* Pittsfield, MA: Printed by Samuel W. Bush, 1829.

Dewey, Mary E., ed. *Life and Letters of Catharine M. Sedgwick.* New York: Harper & Brothers Publishers, 1871.

Drew, Bernard A. *If They Close the Door on You, Go in the Window. Origins of the African American Community in Sheffield, Great Barrington & Stockbridge.* Great Barrington, MA: Attic Revivals Press, 2004.

Egleston, Thomas. *The Life of John Paterson, Major General in the Revolutionary Army.* New York, London: G.P. Putnam's Sons, 1894.

Farrow, Ann, Joel Lang, and Jennifer Frank. *Complicity: How the North Promoted, Prolonged and Profited from Slavery.* New York: Ballantine Books, 2005.

Greene, Evarts B. and Virginia D. Harrington. *American Population Before the Federal Census of 1790.* New York: Columbia University Press, 1932.

Greene, Lorenzo Johnston. *The Negro in Colonial New England: 1620-1776.* New York: Columbia University Press, 1942.

Higginbotham, Jr., A. Leon. *In the Matter of Color: Race and the American Legal Process: the Colonial Period.* New York: Oxford University Press, 1978.

Holland, Josiah Gilbert. *History of Western Massachusetts. The Counties of Hampden, Hampshire, Franklin, and Berkshire. Embracing an Outline, or General History, of the Section, An Account of its Scientific Aspects and Leading Interests, and Separate Histories of its One Hundred Towns.* 2 Vols. Springfield, MA: Samuel Bowles & Company, 1855

Hopkins, Mark. *Early Letters of Mark Hopkins and Others from His Brothers and Their Mother. A Picture of Life in New England from 1770 to 1857.* New York: The John Day Company, 1929.

Hine, Darlene Clark, Elsa Barkley Brown, Rosalyn Terborg-Penn, ed., *Black Women in America: An Historical Encyclopedia.* Volume 8, Bloomington & Indianapolis: Indiana University Press, 1994.

Jones, Electa, *Stockbridge, Past and Present; Or, Records of an Old Mission Station.* Springfield, MA: Samuel Bowles & Company, 1854.

Kaplan, Sidney. *The Black Presence in the Era of the American Revolution, 1777–1800.* New York: The New York Graphic Society, and Smithsonian Institution Press, 1973.

Kelley, Mary. *The Power of Her Sympathy: The Autobiography and Journal of Catharine Maria Sedgwick.* Boston: Massachusetts Historical Society, 1993.

Kenslea, Timothy. *The Sedgwicks in Love: Courtship, Engagement and Marriage in the Early Republic.* Hanover: Northeastern University Press, 2006.

Levinson, David, ed. *African American Heritage in the Upper Housatonic Valley.* Great Barrington, MA: Berkshire Publishing Group, 2006.

Malone, Dumas, ed. *Dictionary of American Biography*, Volume 8, New York: Charles Scribner's Sons, 1935.

Martyn, Charles. *The Life of Artemas Ward.* New York: Printed by Artemas Ward (a descendant of the subject), 1921.

Martineau, Harriet. *Retrospect of Western Travel, Vol. I.* London: Saunders and Otley, 1838.

McManus, Edgar J. *Black Bondage in the North.* Syracuse: Syracuse University Press, 1973.

Melish, Joanne Pope. *Disowning Slavery: Gradual Emancipation and "Race" in New England, 1780–1860.* Ithaca, NY: Cornell University Press, 2000.

Miller, James R. *Early Life in Sheffield Berkshire County, Massachusetts: A Biography of its Ordinary People from Early Times to 1860.* Sheffield, MA: Sheffield Historical Society, 2002.

Moore, George H. *Notes on the History of Slavery in Massachusetts.* New York: D. Appleton & Co., 1866.

Nash, Gary B. *The Forgotten Fifth: African Americans in the Age of Revolution.* Cambridge, MA: Harvard University Press, 2006.

Nell, William C. *The Colored Patriots of the American Revolution, with Sketches of Several Distinguished Colored Persons: to which is Added a Brief Survey of the Condition and Prospects of Colored Americans.* New York: Arno Press and the *New York Times*, 1968 (originally published by Robert F. Wallcut, 1855).

Piersen, William Dillon. *Black Yankees: The Development of an Afro-American Subculture in Eighteenth-Century New England.* Amherst, MA: The University of Massachusetts Press, 1988.

Piper, Emilie, and David Levinson, *One Minute a Free Woman: Elizabeth Freeman and the Struggle for Freedom.* Salisbury, CT: Upper Housatonic Valley National Heritage Area, 2010.

Sedgwick, John. *In My Blood, Six Generations of Madness & Desire in an American Family.* New York: HarperCollins Publishers, 2007.

Sedgwick, Theodore. *The Practicability of the Abolition of Slavery, A Lecture Delivered at the Lyceum in Stockbridge, Massachusetts, February 1831.* New York: Jay Seymour, 1831. (Reprinted by the Cornell University Library Digital Collections).

Taylor, Charles J. *History of Great Barrington (Berkshire County), Massachusetts.* Great Barrington: C.W. Bryan and Company, 1882.

Taylor, Robert J. *Western Massachusetts in the Revolution.* Providence: Brown University Press, 1954.

Welch, Jr., Richard E., *Theodore Sedgwick, Federalist: A Political Portrait.* Middletown, CT: Wesleyan University Press, 1965.

White, Alain C. *The History of the Town of Litchfield, Connecticut, 1720-1920.* Litchfield: Enquirer Print, 1920.

Wilds, Mary. *Mumbet: The Life and Times of Elizabeth Freeman, The True Story of a Slave Who Won Her Freedom.* Greensboro: Avisson Press, 1999.

Williams, George Washington. *History of the Negro Race in America From 1619 to 1880. Negroes as Slaves, As Soldiers, and as Citizens. Together with a Preliminary Consideration of the Unity of the Human Family, an Historical Sketch of Africa, and an Account of the Negro Governments of Sierra Leone and Liberia.* New York: G.P. Putnam's Sons, 1883. (Reprint Edition by Arno Press and *The New York Times,* New York, 1968).

Zilversmit, Arthur. *The First Emancipation: the Abolition of Slavery in the North.* Chicago: The University of Chicago Press, 1967.

ARTICLES, ESSAYS, AND UNPUBLISHED PAPERS:

Blanck, Emily. "Seventeen Eighty-Three: The Turning Point in the Law of Slavery and Freedom in Massachusetts." *The New England Quarterly*, 75, No. 1 (2002): 24–51.

Cassidy, Benjamin, "a Prolific Writer Ahead of Her Time," *The Berkshire Eagle*, March 29, 2019, retrieved January 31, 2020 from: https://www.berkshireeagle.com/stories/catharine-maria-sedgwick-a-prolific-writer-ahead-of-her-time,568971.

Desrochers, Jr., Robert E. "Slave-For-Sale Advertisements and Slavery in Massachusetts, 1704-1781." *William and Mary Quarterly*, July, 2002: 623–664.

Graham, Paul F. "The Life and Times of Elizabeth Freeman" Unpublished paper, December 21, 1981, Sheffield Historical Society.

Ireland, Corydon, "The Rote Notes of Early U.S. Law", *The Harvard Gazette*, online, August 9, 2013, retrieved January 31, 2020 from: https://news.harvard.edu/gazette/story/2013/08/the-rote-notes-of-early-u-s-law/.

King, Jr., Dr. Martin Luther, "I Have a Dream," speech delivered 28 August 1963, at the Lincoln Memorial, Washington, D.C., Retrieved 6 May 2008 from http://www.americanrhetoric.com/speecehes/mlkihaveadream.htm.

Lovejoy, David S. "Samuel Hopkins, Religion, Slavery, and the Revolution." *The New England Quarterly*, XL (1967): 227–243.

MacEacheren, Elaine. "Emancipation of Slavery in Massachusetts: A Reexamination—1770-1790." *The Journal of Negro History*, 55, No. 4 (1970): 289–306.

Malone, Dumas, ed. Biographical portrait of Tapping Reeve (1744–1823). *Dictionary of American Biography*, Volume 8, New York: Charles Scribner's Sons, 1935, 469.

Malone, Dumas, ed. Biographical portrait of Theodore Sedgwick (1746–1813). *Dictionary of American Biography*, Volume 8, New York: Charles Scribner's Sons, 1935, 549.

Malone, Dumas, ed. Biographical portrait of Charles Sedgwick (1613–1656). *Dictionary of American Biography*, Volume 8, New York: Charles Scribner's Sons, 1935, 549.

Rosenthal, Bernard. "Puritan Conscience and New England Slavery." *The New England Quarterly*, 46, no. 1 (1973): 62–81.

Rosenthal, James M. "Free Soil in Berkshire County 1781." *The New England Quarterly*, 10, No. 4 (1937): 781–785.

Sedgwick, Catharine Maria. "Slavery in New England." *Bentley's Miscellany* 34 (1853): 417–424, reprinted by Salem State College at www.salemstate.edu/imc/sedgwick/slavery.html.

Spector, Robert. "The Quock Walker Cases (1781-83): Slavery, its Abolition, and Negro Citizenship in Early Massachusetts." *The Journal of Negro History*, 53, No. 1 (1968): 12–32.

Swan, Jon. "The Slave Who Sued for Freedom," *American Heritage*, 41, No. 2 (1970): 51–55.

Swanson, Eleanor P., "Tapping Reeve," unpublished article, Litchfield Historical Society.

Welch, Richard E. "Mumbet and Judge Sedgwick." *Boston Bar Journal* 8 (1964): 12–19.

Zilversmit, Arthur. "Quok Walker, Mumbet, and Abolition of Slavery in Massachusetts." *The William and Mary Quarterly*, 25, no. 4 (October, 1968): 614–24.

Zilversmit, Arthur. "Mumbet: Folklore and Fact," *Berkshire History*, 1, No. 1 (1971).

Credits

Back Cover: Portrait of Elizabeth 'Mumbet' Freeman (c.1742–1829) 1811 (w/c on ivory) by Susan Anne Livingston Ridley Sedgwick (fl.1811), © Massachusetts Historical Society, Boston, MA, USA/ The Bridgeman Art Library

Chapter ornament: Strelitzias en Ombres Chinoises, Positif et Négatif © Unclesam #6074167. The flower symbolism associated with the bird of paradise flower is freedom, good perspective, and faithfulness. The bird of paradise flower is so-named because of a resemblance to the actual bird of paradise. In South Africa it is commonly known as a "crane" flower.

Index

ABOUT THE AUTHOR

Ben Z. Rose is a New England-based writer whose books focus on inspirational characters in early American history. His first book, *John Stark: Maverick General*, a portrait of the legendary Patriot commander, was chosen by *ForeWord* magazine as a finalist for best biography. In his second book, *Mother of Freedom*, Ben explores the life of Mumbet, the first African American slave to gain her freedom in a court of law based on the principle of general equality. The book was recommended by *Choice Reviews* as "an insightful account of an unusual lawsuit in post-Revolutionary Massachusetts." Ben has been a featured speaker at numerous bookstores, museums, libraries, historical societies, bookstores, and civic groups. Ben and his writing have been featured in the *Boston Globe*, the *Manchester Union Leader*, the *Concord Monitor*, and the *Walloomsack Review*. He has been a guest on New Hampshire and Vermont Public radio. He can be reached at benzrose@msn.com.

A book group discussion outline and other links related to *Mother of Freedom* may be found on the author's website: www.benzrose.com.

Endorsements

You can't go wrong with Bob Hostetler's writing. These prayers are just what every faith-based writer needs.

– **Jerry B. Jenkins**, NY Times bestselling author and founder of the Jerry Jenkins Writers' Guild

Bob Hostetler's *100 Prayers for Writers* is not merely a book–it is a threshold. A sacred, prayer-soaked passage where ink meets Spirit, and the act of writing is transfigured into a holy encounter. With a poet's tenderness and a prophet's fire, Hostetler beckons us to lace our words into the fabric of God's grand narrative. Each prayer thrums with raw honesty, contending with the terror of the blank page and the thrill of divine spark. For writers longing to craft not just with skill but with soul, this book is manna in the wilderness–a Godstorm of inspiration to enflame your art and hallow your calling.

– **Leonard Sweet**, author of *Decoding the Divine* and *Gridiron Gospel*

Prayer is foundational for a writer. When the words won't come, when the answers are all no, and when every other writer on the planet–but you– has a contract, prayer is the lifeline we all need. But sometimes the words to pray fail us. That's where *100 Prayers for Writers* from Bob Hostetler is the book every writer needs. This book will jumpstart your prayers and help you connect to God. More than a dictionary, style guide, or thesaurus, this book is what we will turn to again and again. It will have a place within easy reach on my desk, and will be my first recommendation when writers ask me for books to help them succeed as a writer.

– **Edie Melson**, award-winning writer, host of The Write Conversation blog, and Director of the Blue Ridge Mountains Christian Writers Conference

You should be warned that if you buy the print version of this book, you'll wear it out from use. And yes, it might be cliché to say Hostettler's *100 Prayers* are beautiful and poignant, uplifting and inspiring, but I'm saying it anyway because it's absolutely true. I'll meditate on these prayers daily, and there's an extremely high chance you will as well.

- **James L. Rubart**, Christy Hall of Fame author of *The Five Times I Met Myself*

Prayer is the gateway to creativity. Here is a great way to start your day at the keyboard.

- **Nick Harrison**, author of *Magnificent Prayer* and *Power in the Promises*

This book is a true delight. The contemplations within are a wellspring of inspiration. Highly recommended!

- **Steve Laube**, president of The Steve Laube Agency